THE SUPER SWEATER IDEA BOOK

THE SUPER SWEATER IDEA BOOK

Hundreds of new and exciting ways
to turn sweater fabrics into
unique fashions, home accessories and gifts

GAIL BROWN
and
GAIL HAMILTON

Butterick Publishing

CREDITS

Editors
EVELYN L. BRANNON
CAROL CASTELLANO

Technical Illustrator
PHOEBE GAUGHAN

Fashion Illustrator
JUDY FRANCIS

Photographers
JOCK POTTLE
LOUIS MANSKI
(Color Plates 3, 4, 5, 9, 10, 11 courtesy of Butterick Fashion Marketing Co.)

Book Designer
KATHLEEN F. WESTRAY

Cover Designer
SALLIE BALDWIN

Library of Congress Catalog Card Number: 77-92584
International Standard Book Number: 0-88421-035-9
Copyright © 1978 by Butterick Publishing
161 Sixth Avenue, New York, New York 10013
A Division of American Can Company

All rights reserved. No part of this book may be reproduced in any form or by any electronic or mechanical means, including information storage and retrieval systems, without permission in writing from the publisher, except by a reviewer who may quote brief passages in a review.

PRINTED IN U.S.A.

To Joe Berardino
G. T. H.
and
David
2-5-57 to 11-12-76
G. E. B.

CONTENTS

INTRODUCTION • 9

1 FABRIC AND PATTERN SELECTION • 13
WHAT IS SWEATER FABRIC? • 14
FABRIC STRETCHABILITY, FIT, AND STYLE • 17
BUYER'S CHECKLIST • 32
THE RIGHT PATTERN, THE RIGHT PATTERN SIZE • 32

2 GETTING READY TO SEW • 35
SWEATERS THAT FIT • 35
FABRIC PREPARATION • 40
CUTTING SWEATER FABRICS • 45
MARKING SWEATER FABRICS • 45
SET YOUR MACHINE FOR SWEATER SEWING • 46

3 SWEATER SEWING • 49
SHORTCUT CONSTRUCTION STEPS • 50
SEAMING SWEATER FABRIC • 52
FINISHING EDGES • 55
NECKLINE FINISHES • 64
HEMS AND CUFFS • 74
SWEATER CLOSURES • 79
INVISIBLY STITCHED SWEATER POCKETS • 85

4 SWEATER DESIGN WORKSHOP • 87
SIGNATURED SWEATER CRAFT GARMENTS • 88
HANDCRAFTED DECORATIVE SEAMS • 89
MACHINE-STITCHED DECORATIVE SEAMS • 90
NECKLINE VARIATIONS • 94
SLEEVE VARIATIONS • 98
CLOSURE VARIATIONS • 101
POCKETS • 115
SWEATER CRAFT SMOCKING • 116
EDGING TECHNIQUES • 117
SWEATERS PLUS LEATHER OR FUR • 128
MIX AND MATCH SWEATER AND WOVEN FABRICS • 130
SWEATER STRIPING • 133
SWEATERS: THE FASHIONABLE ALTERNATIVE FOR MOTHERS-TO-BE • 140

5 HAND-KNITTING AND CROCHETING • 141
    Tools for Knitting and Crocheting • 142
    Selecting Sweater Yarns • 144
    Selecting the Stitch Pattern • 145
    Crocheting or Knitting Stitch Gauge • 146
    Crochet or Knit to Fit • 148
    Crochet Basics • 154
    Knitting Basics • 156
    Blocking Sweater Crafts • 161
    Assembling Sweater Craft Garments • 162
    T-Sweater to Crochet or Knit to Fit • 163
    Knit Your Own Ribbing • 163
    Knitting and Crocheting on the Bias • 165
    Woven Half Skirt for Bulky Knits • 166
    Knit Spool Cording • 167

6 NEW SWEATERS FROM OLD: RECYCLING AND RESTYLING • 168
    Borrowed Ribbing • 168
    New Life for a Thrift Shop Special • 170
    Patchwork Sweater Craft Projects • 171
    Sweater Face-Lifts • 174
    Restyling Handmades • 177
    Mending Sweaters • 178

7 MUCH MORE THAN SWEATERS • 181
    Warm and Cosy Accessories • 182
    More Accessory Ideas • 188
    Sweaters Are for Kids • 191
    Is It a Toy? No, It's a Sweater Pillow in Disguise! • 194
    Sweater Your Home • 199
    Sweater Pillows • 200

APPENDIX • 207
ENLARGING OR REDUCING DESIGNS • 209
METRIC EQUIVALENCY CHART • 209
SOURCES OF INFORMATION AND SUPPLIES • 211
INDEX • 213

COLOR PLATES • 105

INTRODUCTION

SWEATERS— AN ANCIENT ART THAT'S THE NEWEST FASHION

A pair of hand-knitted woolen socks were discovered in an ancient Egyptian tomb dated the fourth century B.C. Sweater fabrics, as you can see, have been around for a long, long time. "Knitting has always been used principally for the making of stockings," noted Thérèse de Dillmont in the *Encyclopedia of Needlework* published in the 1800s. The importance of sweater fabrics, both functionally and fashionably, remained minor for hundreds of years.

Sweater fashions as we know them today are the relatively recent result of dramatic technological, economic, and sociological changes.

The first knitting machine was invented in 1589 for sock making by an Englishman, William Lee. He was refused a patent by Queen Elizabeth who feared his invention would put hand knitters out of work. Commercial production of sweater fabrics did not really begin until the Industrial Revolution almost 200 years later. Marc Brunel is credited with introducing in 1774 the first industrial circular knitting machine, the forerunner of today's intricate and multipurpose knitting machines.

The ready-to-wear industry—and sweater popularity along with it—got a big boost during World War I when garment construction methods and machinery were streamlined and production was accelerated. But sweaters were not yet accepted as clothing that could be worn anytime. They were still regarded as "sporty," especially for women, and were worn primarily for golf, tennis, or skiing. In the 1930s the motion picture industry glamourized "sweater girl" stars and pinups—the best remembered is Lana Turner. Sweaters became synonymous with feminine and sexy.

During World War II, casual clothes such as sweaters and slacks became more practical for the multitude of women recruited into the work force. Added to "the sweater fever" was "The Great Sweater," hand-knitted by thousands of volunteers from 1939–1943—in khaki color for soldiers and marines and navy blue for sailors.

"Sweater dressing," however, has been a growing segment of the fashion scene during the past 20 years. The variety of sweater fabrics that are now available—from the laciest crochet-looks to bulky fisherman's cable knits—seems limitless, yet is increasing daily.

Sweater dressing suits today's mobile lifestyles; sweaters are packable, wrinkle-free, comfortable, layerable, seasonless. Until very recently sweaters were considered a "must buy" wardrobe item—unless, of course, you were one of those lucky people with loads of time and hand-knitting or crocheting talents.

The Super Sweater Idea Book is for people who like to wear custom-fit, handmade sweaters but who, like us, are short on time. This book shows you how easy it is to streamline the sewing process with sweater fabrics and special techniques. You'll make sweaters in a fraction of the time usually spent sewing a garment.

The Super Sweater Idea Book shows you the fast, fun, no-fuss ways to make sweaters that fit for your whole family. Whether you're an experienced seamstress or a first timer, the easy-to-follow instructions teach you the sweater sewing basics—from selecting fabric to fit and finishing. You won't need any special sewing machines either. And sweater fabrics you can buy, make, or recycle are readily available.

You'll find unique sweater gifts that can be made in an evening, inexpensively. You'll learn how to restyle and mend sweaters you already own. You'll even learn sweater craft how-tos for making home furnishings that are luxurious and supersoft, and stretch to fit.

If you don't like to fall into the ready-to-wear trap of seeing yourself coming and going, there's a section in this book just for you. It's called the Sweater Design Workshop. With the simple workshop secrets suggested, plus a little imagination and creativity, you can transform any basic sweater into a designer original.

Join the super sweater sewing revolution—it's exciting because the sweaters you make yourself fit better, last longer, cost less, and are *all yours.* Have fun!

—GAIL BROWN and GAIL HAMILTON

CHAPTER **1**

FABRIC AND PATTERN SELECTION

The success of any sweater project depends on the selection and coordination of the sweater fabric with an appropriate sweater style and the correct pattern size. It's easy! Follow these steps for a great sweater look and fit . . . everytime.

- Choose your pattern style.
- Select the perfect sweater fabric. Coordinate the stretchability, type of knit, fiber content, and other fabric characteristics with the pattern style.

- Choose the right pattern size to minimize fitting adjustments later.

Use the Buyer's Checklist (page 32) as a guide when making your in-store decisions.

WHAT IS SWEATER FABRIC?

Technological advances are producing never-before-seen textile machinery and wonder fibers. Just to describe all the sweater knit fabrics currently available could fill an entire book that would be outdated before printing.

Certain characteristics are typically attributed to sweaters: a pronounced stitch and texture, a lofty hand (loft refers to the pile, thickness, and plushness of the fabric), and, of course, stretch. For the sake of simplicity, we'll call fabrics with these characteristics, especially stretch, "sweater fabrics." See the chart, Knit Stitches and Patterns with Sihouette Suggestions, page 20.

Sweater fabrics can stretch in varying degrees to fit a given shape. This stretchability means that sweater craft projects can be made super fast since the time-consuming fitting, seaming, inner-shaping, and closures are unnecessary! You can get spoiled by making sweater craft projects. There have never been fabrics so fashion-right for you, your family, and your home, yet "sew-easy."

Sweater fabrics can be placed in four categories: sweater fabric by the yard, sweater bodies, hand-knitted or crocheted sweater fabric, and recycled sweater fabric. The following discussion of the four types will help you choose the right sweater fabric for your sweater craft project.

◥. SWEATER FABRIC BY THE YARD

Sweater fabric by the yard is available seasonally in most fabric stores and departments. Sweater fabrics are usually single knits, but they can be more stable double knits too. Most commonly, fabrics are folded in half and rolled onto bolts, either split in half lengthwise, with two selvage edges, or in tubular form. (The fabric comes off circular knitting machines in tubular form.) Fiber content varies considerably, but in the moderate price range most fabrics are acrylic or acrylic blends, polyester or polyester blends.

Subject any sweater fabric to do-it-yourself quality testing (see page 32). Remember, it might be worth the extra dollars invested to spend your time sewing a better-quality sweater fabric or knit that won't bag, sag, pill, shrink, or fade.

Most sweater knits by the yard come in economical widths, 54"–68". A woman's classic crewneck, long-sleeved pullover requires about 1 yard. Compare the fabric costs to ready-to-wear sweater price tags: there's a real saving when you sew your own.

Manufacturers and retailers have realized the importance of color-coordinated ribbing or trim for these sweater knits, and sell it by the yard.

If you can't find sweater knits in your area, refer to the mail-order addresses (see page 211).

◥. SWEATER BODIES

A sweater body is a finished "sweater length"—usually the length from the shoulder to the hem. The hem edge is ribbed or has a knitted finish. Sweater bodies can be purchased in tubular form or already split open. You can also purchase sweater bodies in kits.

The finished edge shapes the sweater to fit body curves and eliminates the need for hemming. Imagine the fitting problems you can avoid and the time you can save!

Widths and lengths vary, although most sweater bodies are packaged according to specific sizes and styles. For example, a label might read "Sweater body and trim for a man's turtleneck style up to a size 46." Lay out your pattern on the

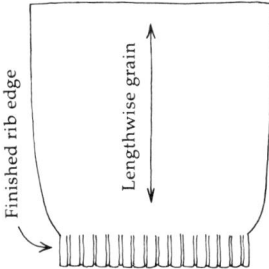

sweater body to make sure you purchase enough to complete your project.

Manufacturers and retailers also sell matching ribbing/trim with sweater bodies for neckline finishing. Ribbing/trim might have two raw edges (apply folded in half) or one finished edge (apply single layer). Turtlenecks require much wider ribbing (4"–10") than crewnecks (1"–4").

◥. HAND-KNITTED OR CROCHETED SWEATER FABRIC

Still can't find a sweater knit? Make your own, either by hand or by machine.

Sweaters can be crocheted and knitted to fit (see Chapter 5, Hand-Knitting and Crocheting) to specific pattern measurements, eliminating the need to cut out the sweater fabric. In manufacturing, sweaters made by this process are called "full fashioned." The full-fashioned technique is great for three-dimensional projects such as socks, hats, or mittens that are shaped as they're knit.

To make cut-and-sewn sweaters, crochet or knit a piece of sweater fabric, then cut out and sew the sweater together. You'll solve the common problem of "I wonder how this sweater I'm knitting or crocheting is going to fit."

Determine the most economical shape and dimension for your pattern layout before proceeding to knit or crochet.

Obviously, this method won't be satisfactory for extremely ravelly stitches or edges that curl excessively and make handling very difficult.

Knitting machines can be set up to knit full-fashioned garments. Because the gauge is consistent, fitting is less of a problem than in hand-knitting or crocheting. Much less time consuming than drafting a project's specified dimensions is simply to knit fabric in a width and length that allows for an economical layout of your pattern. Remember, more tightly knitted sweater fabrics are less likely to ravel and curl. You can use the cut-and-sewn sweater technique to make toys, accessories, and home furnishings too.

RECYCLED SWEATER FABRIC

Go in search of hidden treasures—sweaters you already own! Many sweater craft projects shown in this book were made from such treasures—worn or outdated sweaters tucked away in the back of closets and drawers. Usually parts of these sweaters can be recycled and restyled. (See Chapter 6, New Sweaters from Old: Recycling and Restyling.)

Other inexpensive sources for secondhand sweater fabric are thrift shops, charity bazaars, and flea markets. Not-so-new but good quality sweaters in men's, women's, or children's sizes and styles are available. Prices range from five cents to five dollars! See Buyer's Checklist (page 32) before buying thrift-shop specials.

Here's a hint for sweater bargain hunters. Check "counter appearance" on used sweaters; avoid stretched-out, pilling, or faded fabrics. You may want to use parts of these sweaters, such as the ribbing, to trim sweater knits by the yard (see Borrowed Ribbing, page 168).

Pre-laundering, that is, dry cleaning and/or washing, is suggested for all secondhand sweaters.

FABRIC STRETCHABILITY, FIT, AND STYLE

Determining the stretchability of a sweater fabric is essential to pattern and fabric coordination, and ultimately, to proper fit. If you select a fabric that has moderate stretch for a pattern made "for stretchable knits only" it will result in a too-tight fit. When a pattern calls for a stable double knit, and you choose a very stretchable fabric, your sweater project will be too big and baggy.

Because of their body-revealing traits, sweater fabrics that stretch the most are good choices for bodice garments. Use the more concealing, stable sweater fabrics for skirts or tailored garments.

⚞. COMMERCIAL PATTERN TERMINOLOGY

Commercial patterns give lots of help in coordinating styles and fabrics for sweater sewing. On the front of the pattern envelope, the knit category is given. The possible categories are: For Stretchable Knits Only, For Knits Only, and Recommended For Knits. Patterns also have a stretch gauge on the envelope.

The stretch gauge relates the design of the pattern and the ease allowed for fit to the fabric stretchability, to make coordinating the fabric and the pattern easy. The stretch gauge is based on a standard gauge that uses the terms "stable," "moderate," and "stretchable" to describe the stretchability of knits.

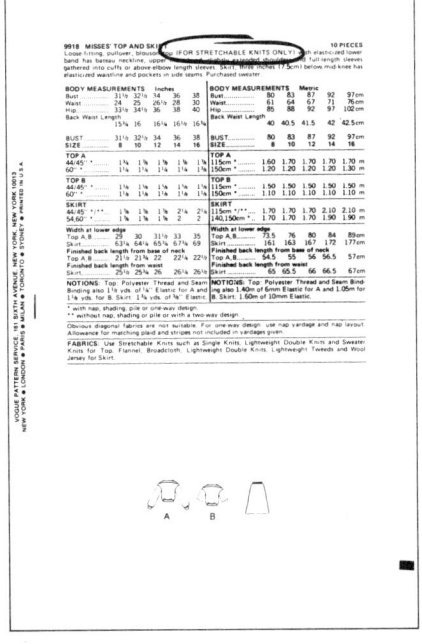

Sweaters can also be categorized by fit. They can be full fit, body fit, or underbody fit. The following chart interrelates all of these terms. *Note:* The ease allowed in patterns varies with the brand and sweater style. Be sure to compare pattern and body measurements (see Sweaters That Fit, page 35).

COMMERCIAL PATTERN TERMINOLOGY

Pattern Category	Stretch Gauge	Fit Category	Means
For Stretchable Knits Only	Very stretchable	Underbody fit	Pattern designed for very stretchable sweater fabrics *only*. Wearing ease and darts have been eliminated; the stretch of the fabric compensates for them. There are few seams. Sweater is cut smaller than body measurements for a tight, body-hugging fit.
For Knits Only	Moderate stretch	Body fit	Pattern designed for moderate to stretchable sweater fabrics. Some or all of the wearing ease has been removed. Darts and fitting lines are usually eliminated. Sweater is cut to body measurements so that fit is close to the body.
Recommended for Knits (or Suitable for Knits)	Stable	Full fit	Pattern designed for stable, less stretchable fabric. The fit is full and not body hugging. Pattern has standard wearing ease allowances.

⌕. COMMERCIAL PATTERN STRETCH GAUGE

To use the stretch gauge on the pattern envelope, place 4" of the crosswise grain of the fabric on the gauge as indicated and stretch. For accuracy, stretch a segment of crosswise grain 10" in from raw edge. If the fabric stretches easily to the mark on the gauge, the fabric is suitable in stretchability for that pattern.

Fabric and Pattern Selection • 19

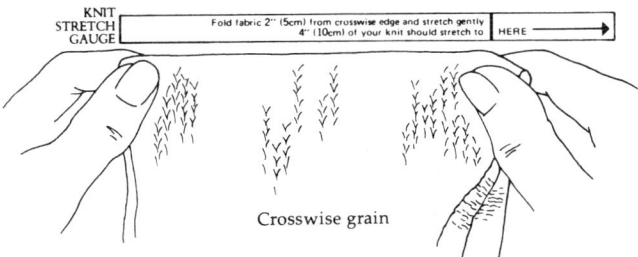

Commercial pattern stretch gauge

To use the general stretch gauge, place the crosswise grain of the fabric on the stretch gauge as indicated and stretch. The area on the gauge into which your fabric stretches easily is labeled with the name that identifies the stretchability of your fabric. *Note:* If the upper edge of your fabric starts to curl, you have stretched the fabric too far.

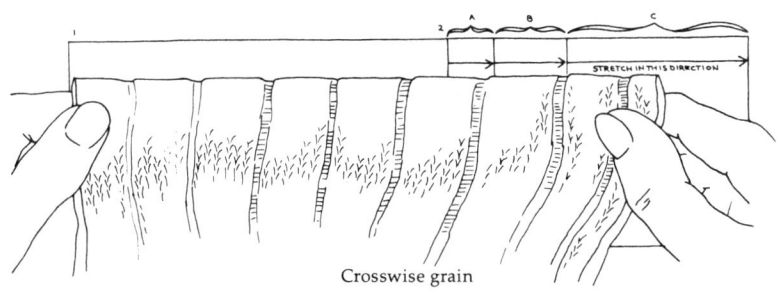

General stretch gauge

KNIT STITCHES AND PATTERNS WITH SILHOUETTE SUGGESTIONS

Since most patterns designed for stretchable knits are sweater looks, coordinating the style with a suitable fabric should be easy. Study ready-to-wear sweaters. You'll notice very simple lines and few pattern pieces. Avoid tailored collars, lapels, and elaborate closures.

Before you choose the fabric, make sure that the weight, texture, bulk, hand, and elasticity lend themselves to your project style. Keep in mind that home furnishings can carry a large stitch pattern and a bulkier, more textured sweater fabric than garments.

Fabric recommendations are given on the back of the pattern envelope. However, different sweater stitches are better suited for different sweater craft projects and can influence fit and style. Most sweaters and sweater fabrics are weft (or crosswise grain) knits. They are constructed much like hand-knitted fabrics. One yarn strand forms continuous rows of loops in the crosswise direction.

There are two types of weft knit—single and double. Single knits are most often used for sweaters because of their greater stretch capabilities. Double knits are more stable because of their double-thickness stitch characteristics.

In warp knits, parallel yarns run lengthwise and interlock into loops.

Because of their structure most sweater fabrics are more stretchable in the crosswise than the lengthwise grain.

The following chart identifies the most common sweater stitches and their structural characteristics, and offers silhouette suggestions. Of course, the stitch characteristic is only one of many sweater fabric components. Variation in yarn size, stretchability, and fiber content can make two fabrics of the same stitch look and act very differently. And the quality of the fabric varies with the yarn weight.

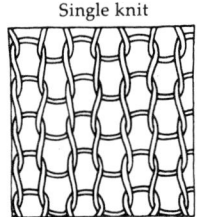

Single knit

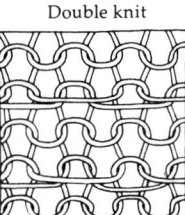

Double knit

KNIT STITCHES AND PATTERNS WITH SILHOUETTE SUGGESTIONS

Double Knit	Stitch Characteristics	Silhouette Suggestions
(Double knit, weft) 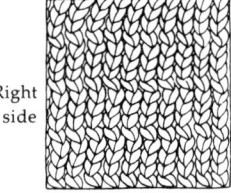 Right side	A double knit is worked on a circular double-needle machine. The yarn loops interlock from front to back. Difficult to distinguish right and wrong sides. Double construction makes these knits stable, with limited stretch capability. Easy to	*Women* Full-fit sweater jackets and pants. In ready-to-wear, coordinated to stretchable sweater knits, skirts, and slacks. *Men* Full fit sweater jackets, leisure suits. *Children* Sweater jackets, pants, dresses. Not rec-

Fabric and Pattern Selection • 21

KNIT STITCHES AND PATTERNS WITH SILHOUETTE SUGGESTIONS

	Double Knit	Stitch Characteristics	Silhouette Suggestions
Wrong side		handle and resistant to bagging or stretching out. Stretchability varies with stitch gauge variations. Compare stretch to stretch gauge before choosing for sweater styles.	ommended for baby clothes because of firm construction. *Home furnishings* If stable, can be made into bedspreads, pillow covers, even simple curtains.

	Jacquard Patterned Knits	Stitch Characteristics	Silhouette Suggestions
Right side	(Single knit, weft)	Various combinations of jersey, purl, and rib stitches. Cable jacquard knits are common and popular. Typified by "fisherman's knit" looks. Patterns most often run vertically. Definite right and wrong sides. Stitch combination usually gives patterned knits a bulkier, loftier hand and look.	*Women* Sweater capes, vests, jackets, coats, sporty sweaters, and dresses. Accessories—hats, scarves, socks, mittens. Trim for plain knits. *Men* Sporty sweaters, vests, hats, scarves. Trim for plain knits. *Children* Lightweight cable knits for sweaters and accessories of all kinds. Baby clothes and blankets. *Home furnishings* Pillows, blankets, afghans, spreads, furniture throws.

	Jersey Knit	Stitch Characteristics	Silhouette Suggestions
Right side	(Single knit, weft)	All loops are pulled to the wrong side of the fabric (looks like purl stitch). Right side looks like hand-knitted stockinette stitch, and has a lengthwise row effect. Stretches across. Edges have tendency to curl. Fabric qualities vary with yarn weight.	*Women* T-shirts, sweater dressing separates. Light to heavyweight sweaters, sweater jackets. *Men* Golf/sport shirts. Light to heavyweight sweaters. *Children* Sweaters. Baby clothes and accessories. *Home furnishings* Patchwork quilts, afghans, pillows.

Wrong side

KNIT STITCHES AND PATTERNS WITH SILHOUETTE SUGGESTIONS

Pile Stretch Knits	Stitch Characteristics	Silhouette Suggestions
(Single knit, weft) (Velours, stretch terry cloth)  (Looped terry) 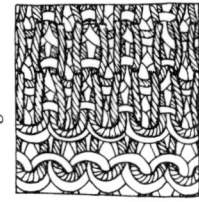 (Sheared velour)	Wrong side looks like jersey stitch. Short pile on the right side—either loops (terry cloth) or sheared loops (velour). An extra filling yarn is added during knitting to form the loops. Fabric is plush and comfortable, although it can require special handling techniques (edges curl, raveling, bulk). Follow one-way or nap layout. Loops may snag easily. Trimmed velours have limited durability.	*Women* Sporty T-shirts and sweaters. Bathing suit coverups. Warm-up jackets and slacks. *Men* Sporty T-shirts and sweaters. Warm-up jackets and slacks. *Children* Pull-on T-shirts. Sweaters, bathing suit coverups. Velour has limited durability so is not usually recommended for children's or babies' playclothes. Soft stretch terry is more durable although it can snag. *Home furnishings* Stretch-to-fit covers and pillows and throws.

(Right side labels on images)

Rib Knit	Stitch Characteristics	Silhouette Suggestions
(Single knit, weft)  Right or wrong side	Alternating jersey and purl stitches. Stitch combinations vary. *Excellent stretch and recovery.* Lofty, bulky hand and look.	*Women* Tight-fitting underbody sweaters and dresses. Trim for sweaters—necklines, cuffs, etc. Accessories—headbands, hats, mittens, socks, scarves, neck warmers. *Men* Slim-fitting pullover styles. Trim for sweaters, accessories (see above). *Children* Stretch-to-fit clothing. Sweaters, hats, mittens, socks. Babies' hats, mittens, socks, jackets. *Home furnishings* Good for "covers"—lamp shades, pillow shams, stretch-to-fit furniture covers.

Fabric and Pattern Selection • 23

KNIT STITCHES AND PATTERNS WITH SILHOUETTE SUGGESTIONS

Purl Knit	Stitch Characteristics	Silhouette Suggestions
(Single knit, weft)  Right or wrong side	Both sides look the same. Loops are pulled in alternate directions to front and back of the fabric. Resembles hand-knit garter stitch. Pronounced horizontal ridges. A lofty, bulky hand and look. Stretch is good in both lengthwise and crosswise directions.	*Women* Sporty sweaters and dresses, shawls, ponchos, vests, tabards. Accessories. *Men* Sporty sweaters (popular for golf and tennis sweaters), vests. Accessories. *Children* Especially good for children's wear because of two-way stretch. Outerwear, sweaters, dresses, accessories. Baby hats, jackets. *Home furnishings* Heavy fabrics made from bulky yarns good for pillows, bedspreads, afghans, throws.

Raschel Knits	Stitch Characteristics	Silhouette Suggestions
(Raschel knit, warp) (Nets, chiffons, piles, etc.)  Right side 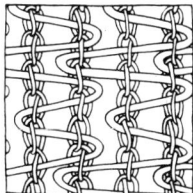 (Magnified view)	Worked continuously with yarns looped in the lengthwise direction. Fabrics vary from lace look to upholstery. Most common is a lacy open structure. Can be identified by chain of fine yarn or thread running in lengthwise direction to stabilize other yarns in open construction. Can be produced only by machine (no hand-crafted counterparts). Stretch varies with denseness, weight. Compare crosswise stretch to stretch gauge of the fabric. Edges may curl and ravel excessively. Can be delicate because of open structure (can pull and snag).	*Women* Open-work for sweaters, tops, dresses. Pile types for sweater coats, jackets. *Men* Pile types for sweater jackets. *Children* Limited use because of relatively delicate structure. *Home furnishings* Open-work for tablecloths, pillow covers, curtains, trims. Pile types for pillows. Test for snagging and pulling before using in heavy-traffic areas.

➤ SWEATER FABRIC FIBER CONTENT

For easy reference, the following chart is limited to the natural and synthetic fibers most commonly found in sweater fabrics and yarns.

Remember when selecting any sweater fabric, that the fiber content affects the finished project's care, durability, stretchability, and fit.

Pre-laundering is suggested for all sweater fabrics: wash or dry clean just as you would the finished project. Yarns, however, are difficult to pre-launder, so follow the final-care instructions on the label.

Blends, or combinations of fibers, are frequently "the best of both worlds." For example, a natural-synthetic fabric or yarn of 40 percent wool and 60 percent polyester maximizes the hand and warmth of wool and the strength and washability of polyester.

Characteristics of a fiber can be altered by the yarn structure, fabric construction, or chemical/heat finish, but the inherent fiber qualities remain.

The fiber's stretch and recovery, or resilience, are most influential in the sweater fabric's finished performance and dictate the completed project's ability to retain the shape and fit properly. A separate column describes the fiber's degree of resiliency. Remember, however, stretch and recovery are subject to the type of knit stitch (see Knit Stitches and Patterns with Silhouette Suggestions, page 20), stitch gauge (very loosely knitted fabric will stretch out more, fabric tightly knitted will stretch less), and the structural quality of the fiber itself. The overall durability and performance of a sweater knit/yarn result from a balance of all the above factors. In fact, one characteristic frequently counteracts another. Hence, if you choose a fiber with poor stretch and recovery, possibly the elasticity of the stitch, e.g., ribbing or lacy crochet, will compensate for the lack of fiber resilience.

SWEATER FABRIC FIBER CONTENT

NATURAL FIBERS

Fiber and Source	Common Sweater-Related Uses	Properties	Stretch and Recovery	Care
Cashmere From the fleece undergrowth produced by cashmere (kashmir) goats	From lightweight to heavy sweater fabrics for men's and women's pullovers and cardigans, some accessories. Blended with wool for luxury sweater jackets and coats. Seldom seen in children's wear because of expense. Yarns—in blends with wool primarily. 100% cashmere rare because of high cost.	Similar to wool, although easily damaged by alkalies. Comfortable in both warm and cold weather. Can be coarse or very soft.	Good to excellent	Follow care instructions for wool.

CAUTION: Yearly production of true cashmere is small, so the fiber can be prohibitively expensive. Refer to cautions given for wool.

Cotton From seed pod of the cotton plant	Used in blends for added strength—both light- and heavyweight garments. Crocheted and lace warm-weather garments. Fine crocheted tablecloths. Sportweight (dress) and rug yarns.	Excellent strength, comfortable, absorbent. Resistant to pilling and static electricity.	Poor to fair	Machine washable and dryable (susceptible to 5 percent shrinkage, so pre-wash). Withstands high-iron temperatures.

CAUTION: Can deteriorate from mildew, and too much sunshine. Tendency to shrink badly unless treated.

NATURAL FIBERS

Fiber and Source	Common Sweater-Related Uses	Properties	Stretch and Recovery	Care
Linen Fiber of flax plant	Used in blends for added strength and texture. Crocheted and lace warm-weather garments. Fine crocheted tablecloths. Yarn blends for dresses, tops, home furnishings.	Excellent strength, very comfortable, absorbent. Resistant to pilling and lint.	Poor	Dry cleaning recommended. If pre-laundered, can be machine washed and dried. Linen is softer if washed. Withstands hot iron setting.

CAUTION: Bright colors might bleed when laundered. Tendency to shrink badly. Can be stiff and wear poorly. Expensive.

| *Mohair* From fleece of the Angora goat | Knitted sweaters and accessories for both men and women, from sportswear to evening fashions. Blended with synthetics and wool for softness and texture. Not common for children's wear—synthetic imitations are less expensive and washable. Yarns—in 100% mohair, 100% kid mohair, combinations of mohair and synthetics. Adaptable to complex yarns and textured fabrics. | Similar to wool. Very resistant to wear and abrasion. Excellent resiliency. High luster. Can be expensive. | Excellent | Follow care instructions for wool. |

CAUTION: Fleece can be matted with too moist, direct steam pressing. Hold iron away from the surface. Refer to cautions given for wool.

NATURAL FIBERS

Fiber and Source	Common Sweater-Related Uses	Properties	Stretch and Recovery	Care
Wool Fiber from sheep fleece	Used in blends for added warmth, comfort, affinity to dyes, elasticity. Heavy- to lightest weight for outerwear, sweater jackets, sweater dresses, home furnishings. Accessories—hats, mittens, scarves, shawls, socks. Yarn blends and 100% types, in range of weights.	Relatively weak, although long wearing. Very comfortable, exceptional absorbency. Versatile in weight, texture, and color. Very moldable; shapes to curves and forms. Requires little pressing.	Excellent	Usually dry clean. If washable, use warm (not hot) water and mild soap. *Do not use chlorine bleach.* Sweaters may require blocking after washing. *Wool-steam iron setting.*

CAUTION: Tendency to shrink and yellow when washed. Susceptible to moths and carpet beetles. May pill. Tendency to stretch when wet. Weakened by sunlight. Some people are allergic to wool.

SYNTHETIC (MAN-MADE) FIBERS

Brand names for each generic synthetic fiber are given. Because knowledge of fiber content is essential to proper care of the completed sweater project, look and ask for labeling on all sweater fabric, yarn, and garments. By law, manufacturers must designate content and care instructions.

Acetate Acele[10] Avicolor[12] Avisco[12] Celanese[7] Chromspun[11] Estron[11]	Limited sweater uses. Some blends for silk-like appearance, luster, and economy. Lightweight jerseys for tops and dresses. Yarn blends for lightweight dresses and tops. Also, "yarn ribbon" for hats, tops, trims, and dresses.	Relatively weak, especially when wet. Tends to hold in body heat. Drapes well and dries quickly. Excellent luster. Good affinity for dyes. Inexpensive. Resistant to moths and mildew.	Poor to fair	Usually dry clean. If washable, wash by hand or set machine on gentle cycle. *Acetates are extremely sensitive to high temperature.* Air dry or tumble dry on low setting. *Use cold or warm water and the coolest iron setting.*

CAUTION: Dyes are subject to atmospheric fading. Loses strength when wet. Weakened by sunlight. Tendency to wrinkle and pill. Melts at high heat. *Acetone (in nail polish remover) dissolves acetate.*

SYNTHETIC (MAN-MADE) FIBERS

Fiber and Source	Common Sweater-Related Uses	Properties	Stretch and Recovery	Care
Acrylic Acrilan[16] Creslan[3] Orlon[10] Zefkrome[9] Zefran[9]	Extensive use in sweater fabrics and yarns. Found in outerwear, often blended with other fibers. Sweaters of all kinds, particularly children's and babies'. Blankets and pile fabrics. Pillows, bedspreads, coverlets, quilts, and furniture throws. Accessories—scarves, hats, mittens, socks. Yarn blends and 100% types of all weights, from baby to bulky yarns.	Quite strong. Very soft hand, excellent "bulking" qualities. Relatively comfortable because of softness, although low absorbency. Quick drying. Wrinkle resistant. Resembles wools, but is washable and less expensive. Good affinity for dyes. Colorfast. Lightweight. Resistant to mildew, moths, chemicals, and sunlight.	Good to excellent	May be dry cleaned, but usually washable. Use warm-water setting and tumble dry. Add fabric softener to the wash-rinse to reduce static electricity. Remove from the dryer as soon as the cycle is complete. Ironing is not necessary. *Avoid too-hot wash water and iron. Press only from the wrong side with steam to prevent shine.*

CAUTION: Susceptible to pilling and static electricity. Heat sensitive. "Remembers" shape, therefore, difficult to block to measurement.

Fiber and Source	Common Sweater-Related Uses	Properties	Stretch and Recovery	Care
Metallic Lurex[9]	Blended with other fibers for fashion accent. Seen in sweater trims and accessories. Shawls and evening wraps. Yarn blended with other fibers for dresses, wraps, accessories.	Weak. If coated with plastic, acetate, or polyester, does not tarnish. Is not affected by salt water, chlorine, or climate. Nonabsorbent. Unique fashion accent—reflects light.	Very poor	Care varies with amount of metallic fiber in the blend. Follow care instructions given. *Do not use hot temperatures for washing or pressing.*

CAUTION: Very weak if not blended with another fiber. Can be irritating to very sensitive skin. May tarnish if not properly coated. Extremely heat sensitive.

Fabric and Pattern Selection • 29

SYNTHETIC (MAN-MADE) FIBERS

Fiber and Source	Common Sweater-Related Uses	Properties	Stretch and Recovery	Care
Modacrylic Dynel[18] Verel[11]	Very limited sweater uses. Most often blended with other fibers, such as wool and acrylic yarns. Yarns blended in very low percentage with other fibers. Most widespread use is for hair imitations, fake furs, and wigs.	Excellent shape retention and elasticity. Quick drying. Resists wrinkling, moths, mildew, chemicals, fire. Nonallergenic. Low absorbency.	Excellent	Care varies with percentage of modacrylic fiber in the blend. Follow care instructions given. *Extremely sensitive to heat. Avoid hot iron.*

CAUTION: Holds body heat. Extremely heat sensitive. *Acetone (in nail polish remover) melts modacrylics.*

Nylon Antron[10] Blue C[16] Caprolan[1] Cedilla[7] Celanese[7] Enkalure[4] Qiana[10] Touch[1]	Often blended with other fibers for strength. Lightweight jerseys. Sporty lightweight sweaters—usually blends with acrylic and wool. "Open work" home furnishings, tablecloths, casement draperies. Yarns blended with orlon and wool for sweaters and dresses.	Exceptional strength. Wrinkle-resistant. Inexpensive. Nonabsorbent; holds body heat. Versatile. Very elastic. Good affinity for dyes. Easy and fast to wash and dry. Resistant to oily stains. Highly resistant to moths and mildew. Abrasion-resistant.	Excellent	Wash often, as soon as soiled. Remove oily stains before washing. Care varies with percentage of nylon in the blend. Follow care instructions on label. Usually machine washable and dryable. Cool water is suggested. Separate colors to avoid graying. Tumble dry and remove before wrinkles set. Add fabric softener to reduce static electricity. *Use the lowest iron setting on the wrong side of the fabric.*

CAUTION: Can be very uncomfortable because of nonabsorbent nature. Tendency to pill, fade, and attract dirt. Melts under high heat. Whites may yellow or gray. Static electricity accumulates in nylon fabrics and yarns. Retains body odors.

SYNTHETIC (MAN-MADE) FIBERS

Fiber and Source	Common Sweater-Related Uses	Properties	Stretch and Recovery	Care
Polyester Avlin[12] Dacron[10] Encron[4] Fortrel[7] Kodel[11] Quintess[17] Trevira[14] Vycron[6]	Used in blends with wool and acrylic, all weights. Also 100% polyester sweater fabric coordinated to double knit sportswear. Limited usage in sweaters because of relatively stiff hand. Yarn blended primarily with wool and acrylic.	Excellent strength. Versatile. Wash and wear, quick drying. Low absorbency. Resistant to wrinkles, stretching, shrinking, abrasion, and moths.	Excellent	Wash by machine or hand. Set on warm water and cool rinse to prevent wrinkles. Tumble or air dry. Remove oily stains before washing. Fabric softener reduces static electricity. *Use a medium-warm steam setting and press on the wrong side to prevent fabric shine.*

CAUTION: Oil may be difficult to remove. Tendency to yellow and gray. Tendency to pill. Accumulates static electricity. Retains body odors. Picks up lint.

Fiber and Source	Common Sweater-Related Uses	Properties	Stretch and Recovery	Care
Rayon (also labeled as viscose on some imported yarns) Avril[12] Beaunit[6] Coloray[8] Englo[4] Fibro[8] Zantrel[4]	Common in blends with orlon, wool, cotton. Uses vary with blend and weight. Yarn blends with metallic, cotton, orlon, in all weights.	Relatively weak fiber, especially when wet. Versatile. Absorbent, soft. Holds in body heat. Good affinity for dyes. Colorfast. Inexpensive.	Poor	Dry cleaning is usually recommended. If machine or hand washing, use mild detergent and gentle cycle. Do not wring, twist, or soak colored fabrics. *Iron on low steam setting. Press on wrong side to prevent shine and discoloration.*

CAUTION: Unless treated, can wrinkle and stretch excessively. Weakened if exposed to light over prolonged period. Low resistance to mildew. Highly flammable.

Fabric and Pattern Selection • 31

SYNTHETIC (MAN-MADE) FIBERS

Fiber and Source	Common Sweater-Related Uses	Properties	Stretch and Recovery	Care
Spandex Lycra[10]	Blended with other fibers, such as wool, rayon, polyester, for added elasticity. Limited sweater uses. Form-fitting tops and sweaters. Primarily for sportswear—skiwear, swimwear.	High strength. Lightweight. Durable. Non-absorbent. Oil repellent.	Excellent	Washable, by hand or machine. Warm-cool water, gentle agitation. Tumble or drip dry. *Avoid chlorine bleach. Iron at low synthetic setting.*

CAUTION: Heat sensitive. May yellow after many launderings or with exposure to light.

Vinyon	Blended with other fibers for heat bonding. Seen most often in imported yarns, combined with nylon and acrylic fibers.	Good strength. Resistant to chemicals and sunlight. Nonflammable. Moth and mildew resistant. Oil repellent.	Good to excellent	Follow care instructions for polyester. Care varies with percentage of vinyon in blend.

CAUTION: Oils that penetrate the fiber itself are hard to remove. Heat sensitive. Accumulates static electricity.

TRADEMARKS:
Fiber groups are registered trademarks of the following companies:
    [1]Allied Chemical
    [2]American Bemberg
    [3]American Cyanamid
    [4]American Enka
    [5]American Manufacturing Co.
    [6]Beaunit Corporation
    [7]Celanese Corporation
    [8]Courtaulds, North America
    [9]Dow Badische
    [10]E. I. DuPont de Nemours
    [11]Eastman Chemical
    [12]FMC Corporation, American Wholesale Division
    [13]Hercules
    [14]Hoechst Fibers
    [15]Hystron
    [16]Monsanto
    [17]Phillips Petroleum
    [18]Union Carbide

BUYER'S CHECKLIST

Ask yourself these questions before you select sweater fabrics.

- Do the fabric stretchability, type of knit, fiber content, and pattern style all coordinate?
- How will the fabric look on me?
- Will it be comfortable to wear?
- Do the fiber content characteristics suit the end use?
- Which is more important . . . appearance or durability?
- What are the care requirements for the fabric? Dry cleaning? Washing?
- If the sweater is to be pulled on and off, is the fabric elastic enough to spring back?
- Does the fabric bag or sag?
- Are both sides of the fabric free of flaws like snags and runs?
- Does the fabric wrinkle? (Wrinkling is seldom a problem with sweater fabric, but crush the fabric in your hand to make sure it doesn't wrinkle too much.)
- Is the grain acceptably straight? Hold the fabric up to the light to see the grain more clearly. (See page 40.)

THE RIGHT PATTERN, THE RIGHT PATTERN SIZE

The most important element in making a sweater that fits is coordinating the stretchability of the fabric with the style of the pattern. After that the project is much easier; fitting is really minimized if the right pattern size is selected. The bust/chest circumference is the most important measurement in pattern selection. Length can be easily adjusted in the pattern fitting before you cut out your sweater project and is a much easier adjustment to make than circumference. If you choose the correct bust/chest size, fitting is usually minimized because the characteristic stretch of the fabric conforms to body contours.

To select the right pattern size, take the measurements indicated in the illustrations and compare them to those on the pattern sizing chart. Find the pattern size that most nearly matches your own measurements.

Fabric and Pattern Selection • 33

COMMERCIAL PATTERN SIZES

(Measurements in inches)

MISSES'

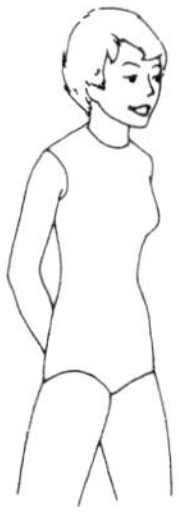

Size	6	8	10	12	14	16	18	20
Bust	30½	31½	32½	34	36	38	40	42
Waist	23	24	25	26½	28	30	32	34
Hip	32½	33½	34½	36	38	40	42	44
Back Waist Length	15½	15¾	16	16¼	16½	16¾	17	17¼

GIRLS'

Size	7	8	10	12	14
Breast	26	27	28½	30	32
Waist	23	23½	24½	25½	26½
Hip	27	28	30	32	34
Back Waist Length	11½	12	12¾	13½	14¼
Approximate Height	50	52	56	58½	61

MEN'S

Size	34	36	38	40	42	44	46	48
Chest	34	36	38	40	42	44	46	48
Waist	28	30	32	34	36	39	42	44
Hip (Seat)	35	37	39	41	43	45	47	49
Neckband	14	14½	15	15½	16	16½	17	17½
Shirt Sleeve	32	32	33	33	34	34	35	35

BOYS' AND TEEN BOYS'

Size	7	8	10	12	14	16	18	20
Chest	26	27	28	30	32	33½	35	36½
Waist	23	24	25	26	27	28	29	30
Hip (Seat)	27	28	29½	31	32½	34	35½	37
Neckband	11¾	12	12½	13	13½	14	14½	15
Approximate Height	48	50	54	58	61	64	66	68

CHILDREN

Children are easy to fit because their bodies are basically straight. Take the child's measurements and compare them to those on the pattern sizing chart. Remember that age does not always correlate to size.

CHILDREN'S MEASUREMENTS
(Measurements in inches)

TODDLERS' Size	½	1	2	3	4		
Breast or Chest	19	20	21	22	23		
Waist	19	19½	20	20½	21		
Approximate Height	28	31	34	37	40		
Finished Dress Length	14	15	16	17	18		

CHILDREN'S Size	2	3	4	5	6	6X
Breast or Chest	21	22	23	24	25	25½
Waist	20	20½	21	21½	22	22½
Hip	—	—	24	25	26	26½
Back Waist Length	8½	9	9½	10	10½	10¾
Approximate Height	35	38	41	44	47	48
Finished Dress Length	18	19	20	22	24	25

CHAPTER 2

GETTING READY TO SEW

You're on your way to creating a unique sweater craft garment. Follow the next steps—preparation of your pattern, fabric, and sewing machine—carefully, and you will make a perfect sweater that fits. The first step is to choose the correct pattern size in order to make minimal fitting alterations.

SWEATERS THAT FIT

Begin by checking the fit, using the following chart.

Fitting Area	Standard Pattern Measurement	Your Measurement	Actual Paper Pattern Measurement	Ease	Alteration
1. Bust (Chest)					
2. Waist					
3. Hip (Seat)					
4. Upper Arm					
5. Back Waist Length					
6. Front Length					
7. Sleeve Length					
8. Back Width					

Standard Pattern Measurement Fill in the standard measurements from the back of the pattern envelope.

Your Measurement Fill in your own measurements. To take measurements, refer to illustrations.

Actual Paper Pattern Measurement Measure the paper pattern at each corresponding point and fill in the measurements of the paper pattern. Remember that the paper pattern represents only half the garment: you have to double the figures so that they can be compared with the

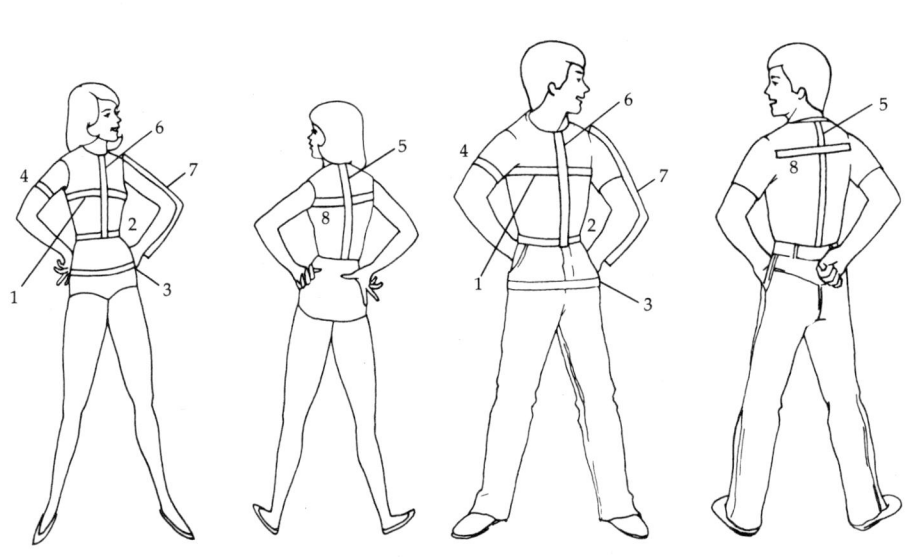

circumference measurements in the other columns. *Do not include pattern seam allowances in your measurements.*

Ease Subtract the Standard Pattern Measurements from the Actual Paper Pattern Measurements to get the wearing ease designed into your particular pattern. The chart Sweater Ease Guidelines relates the sweater fit, fabric stretchability, and wearing ease usually allowed in patterns for knit fabrics (see page 38).

Alteration Subtract Your Measurements from the Actual Paper Pattern Measurements to determine the changes that you must make for perfect fit. Since each change must be distributed around the entire circumference, make only ¼ of the change on each pattern piece. For example, if you must add 1" to the bust, and the pattern represents one half of the garment, you will add ¼" to the front pattern piece and ¼" to the back pattern piece. *Note:* If you have to alter more than a total 2½" in any circumference area, you probably chose the wrong pattern size.

Following is a chart filled in by a woman with measurements typically different from those on the pattern envelope. Her fabric is moderately stretchable, for body fit. First she filled in the measurements from the pattern envelope and her own measurements. Then she wrote in the paper pattern measurements and the ease allowed in the pattern she chose. Lastly, she calculated and filled in the alterations she has to make.

Fitting Area	Standard Pattern Measurement	Your Measurement	Actual Paper Pattern Measurement	Ease	Alteration
1. Bust (Chest)	32½	33	33½	1	½"
2. Waist	25	24	34⅜	—	—
3. Hip (Seat)	34½	35	35½	1	½"
4. Upper Arm		10	15		—
5. Back Waist Length	16	16	16	0	
6. Front Length		15	15		
7. Sleeve Length		21½	21¾		¼"
8. Back Width		15	16½		1½"

Note: Remember, the ease allowed varies with sweater styles. For example, a bell-shaped sleeve might measure 4″–8″ larger than the upper arm to form the style line.

SWEATER EASE GUIDELINES
(Measurements in inches)

Body Circumference	Standard-Full Fit	Body Fit	Underbody Fit
	(Stable sweater fabrics)	(Moderately stretchable fabrics)	(Very stretchable fabrics)
Bust (Chest)	+2 to 4	0 to 2	−2 to 0
Hip (Seat)	+2 to 4	0 to 2	−2 to 0
Waist	+2 to 4	0 to 2	−2 to 0
Upper Arm	+2 to 4	0 to 2	−2 to 0
Back Width	+1 to 2	0 to 1	−1 to 0

◣ PATTERN ADJUSTMENTS

Circumference adjustments are generally done at the side seams.

To increase:

1. Determine the amount you need to increase and make a mark ¼ of that amount outside the cutting line at the side seams of the waistline and hipline.

2. Taper the new cutting line from nothing at the underarm to the adjusted marking at the waistline and hipline.

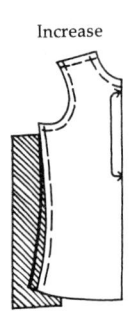

To decrease:

1. Determine the amount you need to decrease and make a mark ¼ of that amount inside the cutting line at the side seams of the waistline and hipline.

2. Continue as you would if you were increasing—tapering from nothing at the underarm to the adjusted markings.

Sometimes you'll need to increase at one point and decrease at another, for instance, a decrease at the waistline and an increase at the hipline. Make one evenly curved line and continue as if both adjustments were the same.

Length adjustments are done on the double horizontal line (lengthening or shortening line) or at the lower edge of the garment.

Increase   Decrease

To lengthen:

1. Determine the amount you need to lengthen by comparing your measurements to the measurements of your pattern.
2. Cut along the adjustment line and place tissue between the pieces you've cut apart.
3. Pin in place, separating them the amount of the adjustment equally all the way across.
4. Secure with tape.
5. Redraw the interrupted lines at the seams.

To shorten:

1. Determine the amount you need to shorten by comparing your measurements to the measurements of your pattern.
2. Draw a line above and parallel to the lengthening and shortening line.
3. Crease the pattern along the adjustment line and fold it up so that the crease meets the line you drew.
4. Pin in place and secure with tape.
5. Redraw the interrupted lines at the side seams and your adjustment is complete.

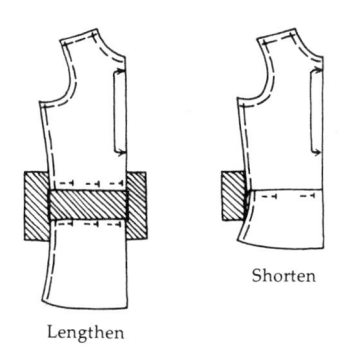

Pattern pieces with little or no shaping have the adjustment line at the lower edge. Simply add on or take away the amount needed an equal distance all around. If you are adding on, simply extend the side seams at the same angle they're at above the adjustment.

As a fitting precaution, compare the sweater pattern to a ready-made that fits and is similar in stretchability to your fabric—*before cutting.* Make the alterations necessary in the paper pattern. Cut the sweater, pin baste, and try on. Make any final changes in the fit.

✎. PATTERN ADJUSTMENTS FOR CHILDREN

(See the chart, Children's Measurements, page 34.) Size adjustments for children should also be made along seam lines. If the size has to be adjusted more than ½" on each seam, the pattern you've purchased is too small or too large.

Double check the pattern size with a ready-made that fits and is of comparable stretchability to the fabric you've chosen. *Note:* Children grow faster in height and arm length than in body and shoulder width. Build in "grow room" by allowing for extra length in the sleeves and bodice.

➤ MAKE YOUR OWN PERFECT-FIT PATTERN

Here is a sure-fire way to sew a sweater that fits! Make a pattern from a favorite-fitting ready-to-wear sweater.

There are a couple of ways to carbon copy the fit favorite. If the sweater is worn out, simply cut it apart. Cut along seam lines and save trimming, ribbing, etc. Transfer the sweater fabric "pattern" by tracing it onto nonwoven interfacing or butcher paper. Don't forget to add 5/8" seam allowances. Make patterns for ribbing, bands, and collars too.

If you don't want to cut up the sweater, try this tracing method. Lay the sweater out, one section at a time, on nonwoven interfacing or butcher paper. Trace around the sweater following the seam lines. Transfer grain lines too.

Although the backs and fronts of most sweaters are the same size, trace both for neckline differences. Sleeves are difficult to trace, but not impossible. Fold the sleeve in half lengthwise and trace around the half sleeve. Then fold the tracing over to double the width and duplicate the sweater sleeve exactly.

Fold all pattern pieces in half lengthwise to "true-up" any size discrepancies between the two sides. Add 5/8" seam allowances.

You'll find this sweater pattern indispensable. You can make dozens of sweaters from this basic design that fits. Sewing for the man in your life? This is a super sneaky way to surprise him with a sweater gift that fits! *Note:* For proper fit, the stretchability of the sweater fabric must be similar to that of the sweater from which the pattern was traced. You can double-check commercial pattern sizing with this basic perfect fit pattern too.

THE BASIC SWEATER PATTERN

Once you've developed a basic pattern that fits—for any member of the family—save it! Several different sweaters can be made from this basic pattern simply by varying fabric, neck-lines, sleeves, trim, etc. (see Chapter 4, Sweater Design Workshop). The basic pattern will last longer if it's transferred to butcher paper or ironed to nonwoven fusible interfacing.

FABRIC PREPARATION

Pre-launder all sweater fabrics just as you would the finished garment or craft. If the fabric is tubular, slit along the lengthwise knitted rib line before laundering.

Unlike woven fabrics, sweater fabrics cannot be straightened by tearing or pulling a thread. But knits do have a grain, that is, a lengthwise "rib" row and crosswise "course" that lie at right angles to each other. Follow these stitch lines with your eye to determine if the fabric is even. If it is slightly crooked, pull the fabric "on grain."

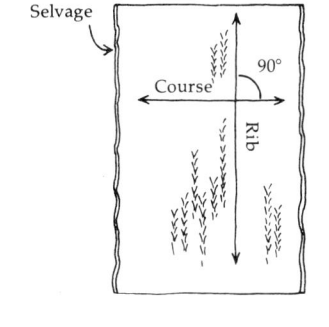

To straighten the lengthwise folds and ends of sweater fabrics, baste along the rib and course lines. Selvage edges aren't always accurate guides for the lengthwise grain on sweater fabrics because they can be pulled and wavy. Follow a lengthwise rib a few inches in from the selvage edge.

Fold the fabric in half lengthwise along the rib basting line. Then align the course basting lines. Next, trim to straighten the fabric ends where necessary. Although the fabric is folded in half for straightening, most heavy sweater fabrics must be single layer for cutting out.

If the sweater fabric is not straightened, the sweater craft garment could possibly be cut off grain which causes twisting, poor fit, and uneven design/stitch lines.

◣. PATTERN LAYOUT

After you straighten out the fabric, fold it for your pattern layout. Commercial pattern instructions give layouts for different fabric widths.

There are some general rules to help you shorten your layout and cutting time:
• Cut out heavy, bulky, or lacy sweater fabrics in a single layer to make cutting and alignment of grain lines easier. However, when you cut out pieces single layer, be sure to "flop" pattern pieces so you have a right and a left side.

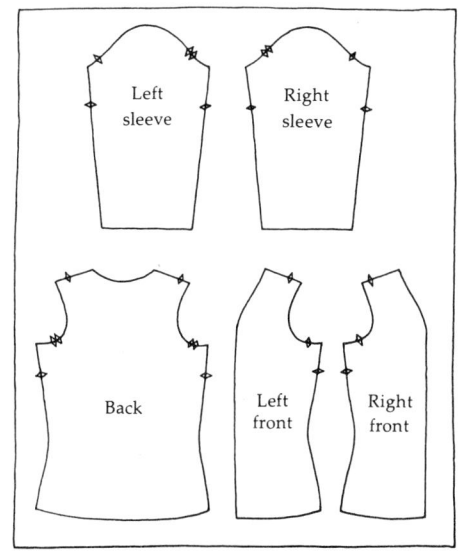

Single layer

- For a pullover style, you need two folded edges for the pattern layout. Fold the fabric selvages in half lengthwise along rib rows.

- With cardigan styles, fold the fabric in half lengthwise along a rib row (only one folded edge is necessary).

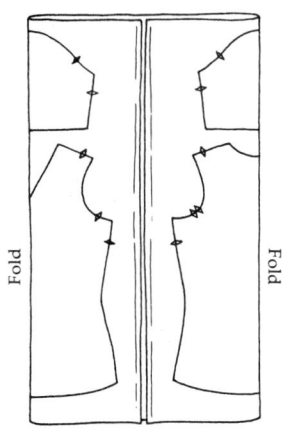

Pullover

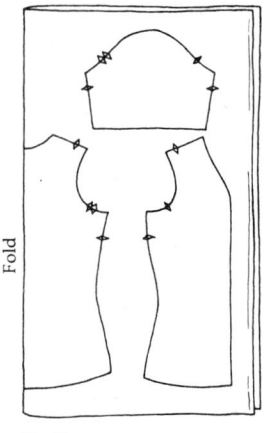

Cardigan

- Some sweater styles and large sizes might require extra wide double layer layouts. Fold the fabric in half along the crosswise course.

Remember that the fabric fold should always be on a grain line. The folded edge, rather than the selvage edges, should be the guideline for straight-grain pattern layout.

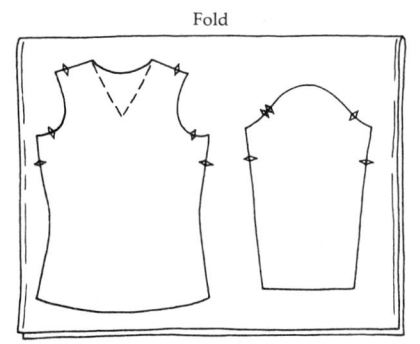

Because of sweater fabric stretch and bulk it's easier to work with patterns cut from butcher paper or nonwoven interfacing. Or you can reinforce tissue patterns with nonwoven fusible interfacing. Regular tissue patterns tear when pinned to soft, lofty sweater fabrics.

Use extra-long pins when you lay out sweater patterns. If pinning is difficult, use dressmaking weights to hold the pattern pieces in place. Dressmaking weights can be purchased in most fabric stores, but small bowls are less expensive and just as functional.

Wide double layer layout

Do not let the fabric hang over the edge of the table or bed while you're laying out the pattern or cutting. If the fabric is stretched out, the grain and fit will be distorted.

Some sweater fabrics have a brushed surface or obvious one-way stitch/design that requires a layout for napped or one-way design fabrics. Commercial patterns give instructions for these fabric variations. For striped fabric layouts, see page 133.

SWEATER FABRIC BY THE YARD (see page 14)

If the fabric is tubular, it is joined by a lengthwise knitted rib. Cut apart along this rib. Straighten the course edges (see page 40). Fold for cardigan (one folded edge) or pullover (two folded edges) style.

SWEATER BODIES (see page 15)

Cut apart along the lengthwise knitted rib if the sweater body is tubular. Straightening the course edges of sweater bodies isn't necessary because of the finished hem edge. Lay out for cardigan (one folded edge) or pullover (double layer).

Stretch out the finished rib edge to form a straight line with the lengthwise rib. Use dressmaking weights or pins to hold the ribbed edge in place while you're cutting. When the edge springs back to the original shape, it will fit to the body contours. It might be helpful to cut out sweater bodies single layer.

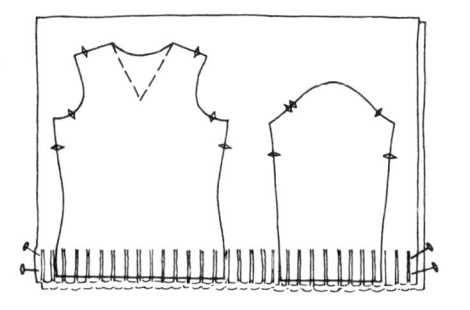

Lay out the pattern so that all hem edges align with the finished sweater body edge (hem allowances are eliminated).

Be certain to check the length of each piece before cutting—the finished hem edge makes altering length difficult.

HAND-KNITTED OR CROCHETED SWEATER FABRIC (see page 15)

The layout varies with the length and width of the crocheted or knitted sweater fabric, but to minimize waste make your fabric only as wide as the widest pattern piece. Lay out patterns in a lengthwise row. Hand-knitted and crocheted fabrics have easily recognizable ribs and courses. Align the pattern's lengthwise and crosswise grain lines with these stitch directions.

RECYCLED SWEATER FABRIC (see page 16)

Cut the sweater apart along seam lines. All fabric to be recycled should be flat and a single layer. Lay the pattern pieces over corresponding sweater pieces. *Caution:* Don't forget to "flop" pattern pieces so that a right and a left sleeve, front and back bodice, etc., will be cut. Save all ribbing, trim, and pockets for finishing.

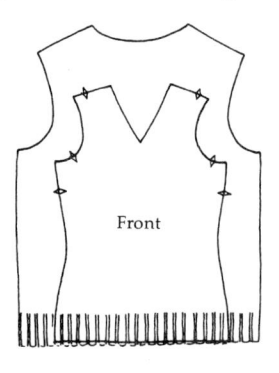

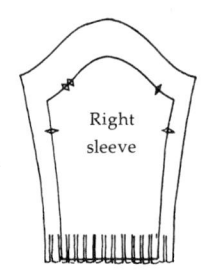

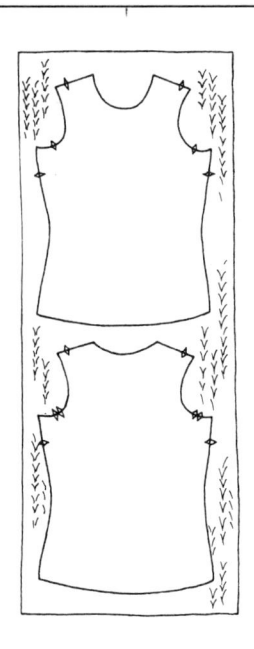

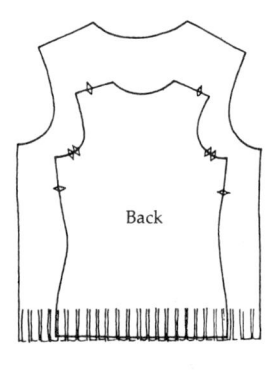

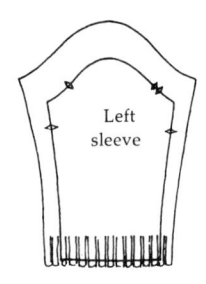

Front

Back

Right sleeve

Left sleeve

⌦. SPECIAL LAYOUT FOR SIDE SEAMLESS CARDIGAN

When you work with heavy sweater fabric, bulk can be a problem. Here's a simple solution: eliminate cardigan side seam bulk in a jiffy with this layout. The side seam fitting contours are eliminated too, so the sweater silhouette will be fairly straight.

Overlap pattern side seams at the hipline and underarm. The side edges will not meet through the waistline area.

Place the center back of the pattern on the fabric fold. When you cut out the new pattern there will be no more side seam.

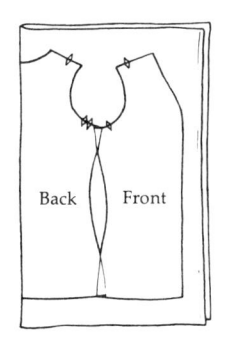

To make this new pattern more durable for re-use and to make handling easier, transfer it to nonwoven interfacing or butcher paper.

CUTTING SWEATER FABRICS

Accurate cutting means easier-to-sew, better-fitting sweaters. Here are a few how-tos for cutting "on line":

- Always keep the sweater fabric flat on the cutting surface, not hanging over the edge.
- If the fabric is difficult to cut double layer, change to a single layer layout.
- Use sharp shears designed for knits. Pinking and scalloped blade shears aren't necessary for sweater fabrics, and they don't produce a sharply cut edge.
- Hold one hand on the pattern for control as you cut out the fabric. You can use dressmaking weights too to hold the pattern in place on the fabric.

MARKING SWEATER FABRICS

Since sweater patterns seldom have any darts or inner construction, marking is not often needed. However, to transfer pocket, button, and buttonhole placements, use tailor tacks, pin

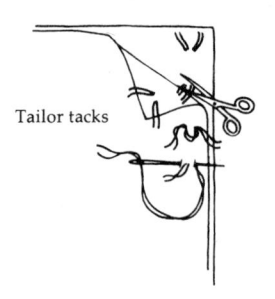

Tailor tacks

markings, or basting. Tracing paper and chalk won't work on sweater fabrics because their surfaces are not smooth or firm enough for markings to be transferred evenly or clearly.

SET YOUR MACHINE FOR SWEATER SEWING

Whether you own a vintage treadle machine or the latest stretch stitch model, you can sew sweater fabrics. Making a few minor machine adjustments will prevent sweater stitching problems.

Of course, you should always start with a clean, well-oiled machine!

◥. SEWING MACHINE ADJUSTMENTS

Test stitch on two 6" × 6" swatches of your sweater fabric.

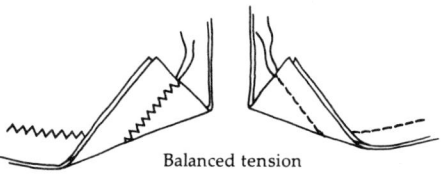

Balanced tension

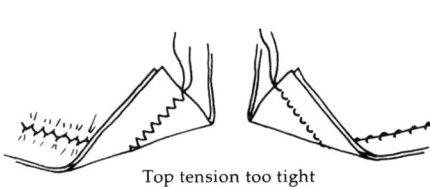

Top tension too tight

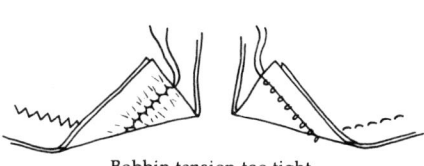

Bobbin tension too tight

If necessary, make the following adjustments.

TENSION

Look at your machine stitch. Does it look the same on both sides? If not, you need to balance your machine tension. Balanced tension is stronger and withstands stretching of sweater seams. Both needle and bobbin thread should meet and interlock in the center of the fabric. Adjust the tension dial to achieve this stronger balanced stitch. *Note:* Before making any tension adjustments, lower machine presser foot, then turn tension dial.

Sewing machine tension can also be balanced by adjusting the bobbin screw or dial. This step should be the "last resort," however, because bobbin tension adjustments should be made only by experienced seamstresses or machine mechanics. *Note:* Check your machine manual for location of tension dial and bobbin screw or dial.

STITCH LENGTH

Recommended stitch length for sewing sweaters is 8–10 stitches per inch, longer than usually specified. Sweater fabric stretches less when stitched with this longer straight stitch.

After testing on a sample sweater swatch for stretching, strength, appearance, etc., adjust zig-zag or stretch stitch length.

NEEDLES AND THREAD

Man-made fibers tend to dull sewing machine needles. Change your needle frequently to prevent skipped stitches. Ballpoint needles are excellent, especially those "banded" for sewing knits because they will not pierce or break synthetic sweater knit fibers. Synthetic thread is recommended for sewing most sweater knits; it gives with the fabric. Choose a lightweight thread to prevent bulky seams.

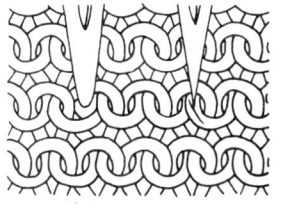

Ballpoint needle   Regular needle

PRESSER FOOT

The presser foot pressure can be adjusted by turning a dial or knob. Check your sewing machine manual or ask a sewing machine mechanic to locate this knob for you. Thin, lightweight sweater knits require more pressure. Bulky sweater knits require less pressure. Cellophane tape over the toes of the presser foot helps to eliminate catching of bulky, loosely knitted sweater knits.

THROAT PLATE

Change to the throat plate and foot designed respectively for straight or zig-zag stitching (stretch, decorative, etc.).

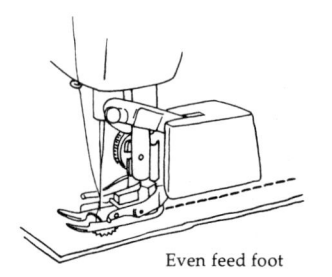

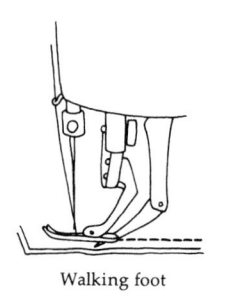

FOOT ATTACHMENTS

If puckering, top seam stretching, or slipping occurs, use an even feed, walking, or roller foot. Some newer machine models are equipped with these attachments, but you can also purchase them separately and inexpensively. Ask about these attachments at your sewing machine dealer or fabric store. Attachments can also be found in the notions department of fabric stores. Be sure to match attachments to sewing machine brand, model, and needle.

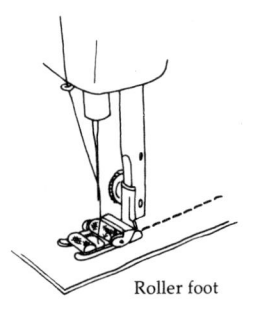

Even feed foot

Walking foot

Roller foot

CHAPTER 3

SWEATER SEWING

It's time to sew the sweater together. This chapter contains step-by-step instructions for sewing just about every style sweater—crewnecks, V-necks, turtlenecks, just to name a few. There are also lots of variations for necklines, edgings, closures, seams, hems, and cuffs. (Refer to Chapter 4, Sweater Design Workshop, for other exciting sweater ideas.) One of the most important features are the shortcut construction steps borrowed from ready-to-wear manufacturers, which will make sewing sweaters an enjoyable, easy, successful activity.

SHORTCUT CONSTRUCTION STEPS

There are several steps that manufacturers follow to make sweaters quickly and easily. You, the home sewer, can follow them, too, to sew professional-looking, well-fitting garments.

✂. CREWNECK, BOATNECK, MOCK TURTLE, AND TURTLENECK SWEATERS

1. Stitch one shoulder seam.
• See Sweater Seams, page 53.
2. Finish neckline with ribbing, binding, or trim. Allow the finish to extend ½" beyond the unsewn shoulder seam.
• See Ribbing—the All-Purpose Edging, page 55.
• See Binding, page 57.
• See Braid or Ribbon Edging, page 58.
3. Sew second shoulder seam. To "hide" the seam, hand stitch inside to the neckline ribbing/trim.

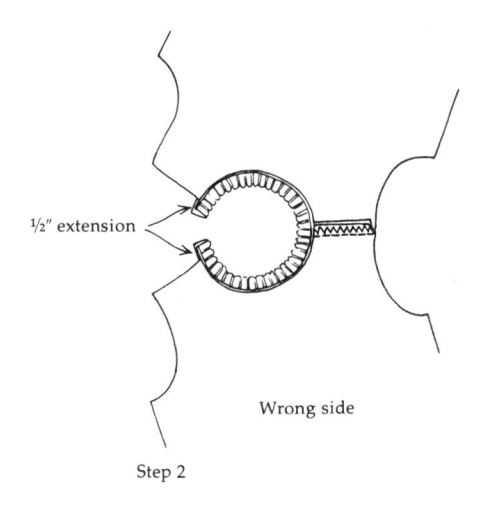

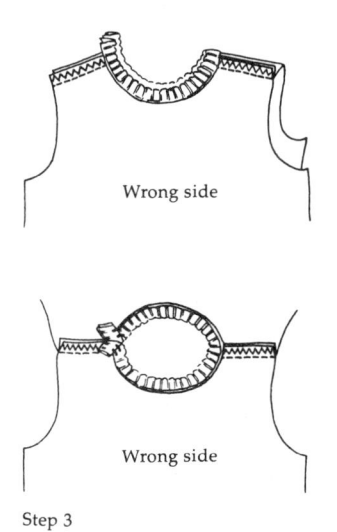

½" extension

Wrong side

Step 2

Wrong side

Wrong side

Step 3

Sweater Sewing • 51

4. Finish armscye with ribbing, binding, or trim. Or, set in sleeves. Apply sleeve hem finish before setting in sleeves.

5. Stitch side seams, matching both sleeve and hem edges. Stitch from hem edge to underarm seam to sleeve hem (directional stitching) to keep hem edges evenly matched.

6. *Optional* If your sweater project does not have a prefinished hem (such as on a sweater body), complete the garment by hemming.
- See Hems and Cuffs, page 74.

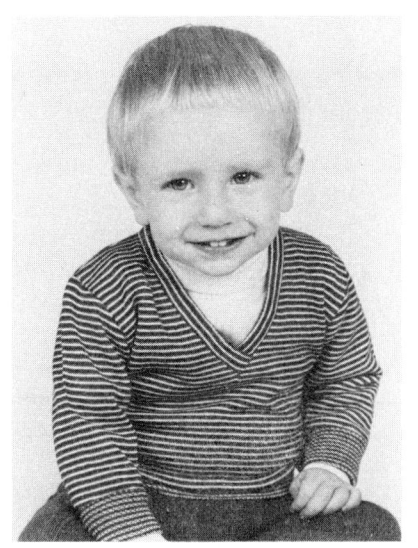

✄. V-NECK SWEATERS

1. Stitch both shoulder seams.
- See Sweater Seams, page 53.
2. Finish neckline.
- See Mitered V, page 67.
- See Lapped V, page 69.

Continue as in Steps 4, 5, 6 of shortcut construction steps for Crewneck, Boatneck, Mock Turtle, and Turtleneck Sweaters (see page 50).

➘. CARDIGANS AND ANY FRONT CLOSURE STYLES

1. Stitch both shoulder seams.
   - See Sweater Seams, page 53.
2. Hem if you are not using fabric with a prefinished hem such as a sweater body.
   - See Hems and Cuffs, page 74.
3. Apply neckline and front edge finish.
   - See Cardigan Sweaters, page 71.

Continue as in Steps 4 and 5 of shortcut construction steps for Crewneck, Boatneck, Mock Turtle, and Turtleneck Sweaters (see page 50).

SEAMING SWEATER FABRIC

The desired result of a sweater craft project is a well-fitting garment with smooth seams and edges. The stretchability of sweater fabrics demands care in sewing seams and finishing edges to avoid stretched-out or wavy lines. One way to keep seams streamlined and sleek is to hem before you sew the seam (see page 74). The seaming techniques given below make sweater seaming easy and ensure professional-looking results.

➘. EASE PLUS

"Ease plus" is the secret to sewing sweater craft items. Sweater seams can stretch out and become uneven, an undesirable look for any sweater craft project. This technique is borrowed from ready-to-wear manufacturers and makes sweater seaming a cinch! If you've never sewn sweater knits before, stage a few test runs on sample swatches.

By making a few minor adjustments on your machine and learning the ease plus technique, you can solve the sweater seam stretch problem.

1. Make the machine adjustments (see page 46 for details).
2. Instead of letting the machine feed dog regulate the flow of fabric under the foot, evenly "force feed" the sweater fabric (top and bottom fabric layers) as you stitch. Pushing the fabric layers between the foot and feed dog prevents stretching of sweater knit seams and hems. Sew ease plus with a 5/8" seam allowance. Trim excess fabric after stitching.

Ease plus

SWEATER SEAMS

There are three sweater seaming methods designed to make seams flat, smooth, and durable. Use ease plus for each of them.

Straight stitch along seam line. With seam allowances still together, stitch again 1/4" away from first stitching. Trim excess seam allowance.

Straight stitch

Straight stitch along seam line. With seam allowances still together, use a *zig-zag* or *multiple zig-zag* (also called the three-step zig-zag) alongside the first stitching. Use a medium to wide zig-zag and a medium stitch length. Trim excess seam allowance.

Straight stitch and zig-zag

Use an *overlock* or *stretch stitch* which seams and overcasts simultaneously. Trim seam allowance. This seam is the most elastic but is difficult to rip out.

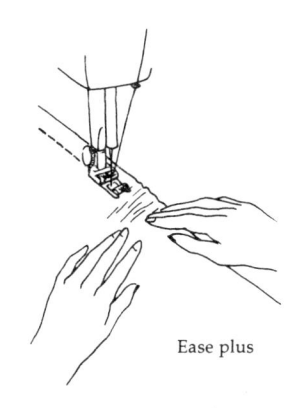

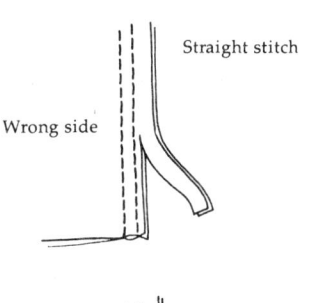

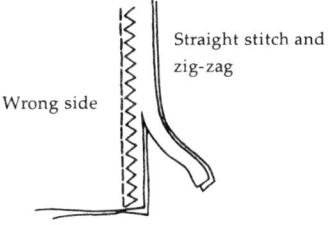

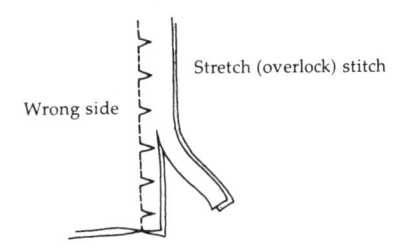

Stretch (overlock) stitch

You do not need a stretch stitch sewing machine to make sweater craft garments. Seams done by the straight stitch or straight stitch/zig-zag methods are effective.

Stitch pre-washed narrow twill tape into the seam to prevent stretching. As an alternative to twill tape, use a raveled yarn from the sweater fabric. This technique is especially good when working with loosely knitted sweater fabric. Insert twill tape or yarn strands in seams and cut them short of the seam intersection to minimize bulk.

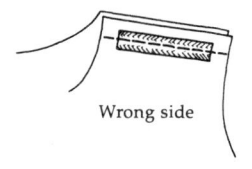

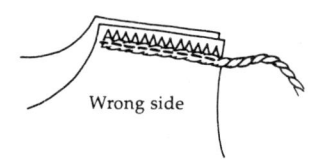

Wrong side

Wrong side

⌇. DEALING WITH BULK

The stretch texture and pronounced stitch define sweater knits in the multitude of fabrics available today. Yet these same qualities can combine to create a sewing problem—bulk. Bulk is the arch enemy of sweater craft projects. There are some easy ways to prevent unwanted bulk from ruining the professional look and smooth fit of your sweater projects.

AVOIDING BULK IN SWEATER SEAMS

- If the seams are pressed open, clip away all the allowances at a 45° angle. Stitch the joining seam.
- If the intersecting seams are double stitched and trimmed (as shown on page 53), simply turn them in opposite directions before joining.
- Join ribbing/trim at center back, rather than at shoulder seams.

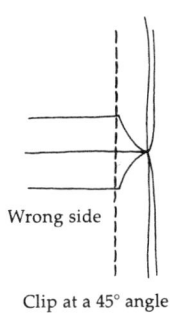

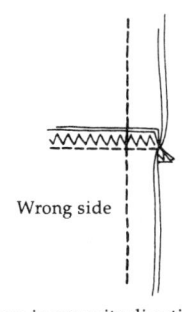

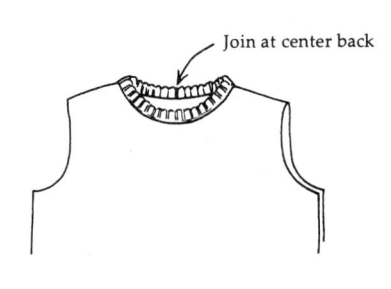

Wrong side

Clip at a 45° angle

Wrong side

Turn in opposite directions

Join at center back

FINISHING EDGES

Sweater edges offer infinite opportunities for creativity and variety in design. You can make your sweater simple or ornate, classic or modern. Add ribbing, braid, or binding for decorative touches, or finish stylishly with elasticized edges. There is no end to the possibilities!

◣. RIBBING—THE ALL-PURPOSE EDGING

Ribbing isn't just for sweaters—it is trimming more and more garments of all kinds. Where does ribbing go? On collars and necklines, on hems and sleeve edges, on jacket bottoms, on hats, gloves, booties, and pockets.

Select ribbing that is not too much heavier or lighter than the fabric it will trim. The care requirements should be the same as for the garment fabric. Don't put a "dry clean only" ribbing with a washable jacket! Use a single thickness ribbing for lighter-weight fabrics and a double thickness for heavier fabrics.

The ribbing is generally cut smaller than the garment so that it hugs the body. Try the ribbing on the respective body area. For cuffs, try it on the hand; for pullover styles, try it over the head; for ankles, try it over the foot; and for hipline, try it over the hips.

RIBBING APPLIED TO HEM EDGE

1. Cut the ribbing to hug the body area it will fit.
2. Distribute the ease along the ribbing and pin in place.
3. Sew with the ribbing side up. Use one of the sweater seams described on page 53. Stretch this seam only enough to give the sweater enough elasticity to be pulled on and to fit the body contours.

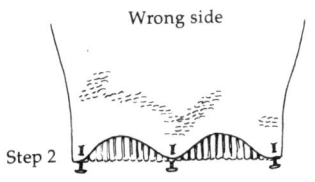

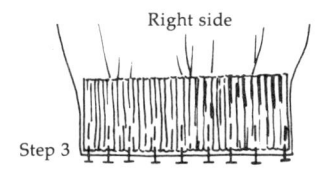

RIBBING AS BINDING

Use on neckline and front edges. This technique minimizes bulk and conceals the seams.

1. Trim away seam allowances on all edges to be bound. Lap the wrong side of the ribbing over ½" of the sweater on the wrong side of the sweater.
2. Use a straight stitch. Stitch, easing the sweater to the ribbing.
3. Turn the ribbing to the right side of the sweater to enclose the seam allowance.
4. Topstitch the ribbing in place close to the edge of the ribbing. Distribute the ease evenly, stretching outer edge of the ribbing to accommodate curved areas. *Note:* When using this technique on the neckline of a cardigan or V-neck sweater, always stitch from the center back to the front on each side. See Cardigan Sweaters, page 71, and V-neck Sweaters, page 67.

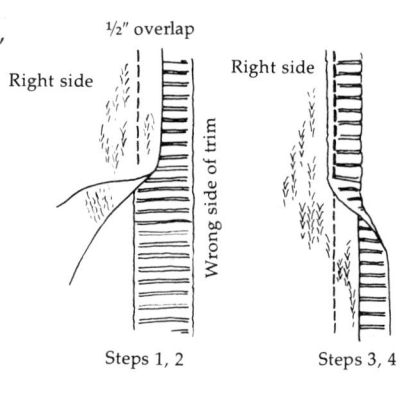

MITERING

Try this easy mitering technique when you're ribbing or binding sweaters with a V or square neck. Mitering is seaming diagonally at a corner. A miter shapes the hem ribbing or binding around a corner with minimum bulk.

1. Encase raw edges of the sweater with ribbing/trim, wrong sides of trim out. Pin out fullness diagonally (45° angle) at each corner on both sides.

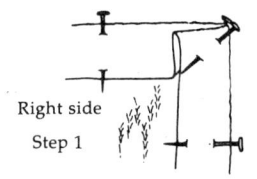

2. Remove trim from garment, leaving diagonal pins at corners. Fold trim, right sides together; mark the V formed by pins.

3. Stitch the V to make each miter. Use a short stitch length (12–15 stitches per inch). Take 2–3 stitches diagonally across point. Trim close to stitching.

4. Turn the mitered seams to the inside. Steam press. The trim is ready to be sewn to the garment, either with topstitching (for ribbing/trim with finished edge) or seaming with an overlock stitch (for ribbing/trim with raw edge).

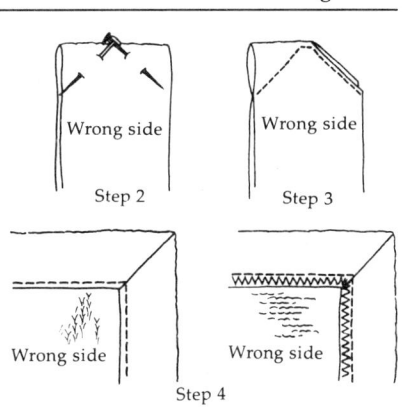

BINDING

Binding is a professional finishing touch for any sweater! This quick technique reduces bulk and makes garments more durable through wearing and washing. Want to mix and match your wardrobe? Binding is a great way to color coordinate separates whether knits, wovens, or combinations of the two.

Binding can be used instead of a hem, a facing, or a lining to finish almost any edge. It can shorten your sewing time. Where can you use binding? On necklines and cardigan fronts, on armscye edges, on pocket tops, on hems, and lots more. Remember that the binding must stretch enough to allow the sweater to be put on. Take special care in deciding what kind of binding to use and where to put it. Test your binding for stretchability and recovery.

If it is necessary to make square corners in your binding, use the technique for mitering, page 56.

STITCH IN THE DITCH BINDING

1. Cut fabric strips 2½ times as wide as the desired width of the finished binding.
• Cut knits and sweater fabrics on the crosswise or bias grain.
• Cut woven fabrics on the bias.
• The length you need depends on the number and length of edges to be bound.

58 • THE SUPER SWEATER IDEA BOOK

You may need to make continuous bias strips. Simply seam the bias strips together with the joining seam on the bias grain. Press seam open.

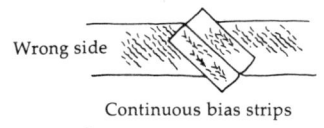

Wrong side

Continuous bias strips

2. Trim off the pattern seam allowances of the edges to be bound. Make new seam allowances equal to the finished binding width (e.g., ½" seam allowance, ½" binding).

3. Place binding strips along the raw edge, right sides together. Straight stitch along the new seam allowance line.

4. Turn the binding strip to

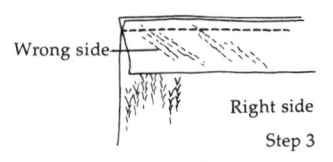

Wrong side
Right side
Step 3

the wrong side of the garment enclosing the seam edges. Do not press this flat since a soft roll will make the binding look best.

5. Stitch in the ditch. Attach the zipper foot. Lengthen machine stitch to 8 stitches per inch. This is the crucial step that eliminates the need for hand stitching! Stitch by machine with matching thread in the groove between the binding and fabric. Separate the seam with your fingers as you sew so that stitching will land directly into the seam "well."

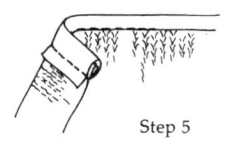

Step 5

6. Trim away excess binding fabric on the inside of the garment.

Note: Loosely knitted sweater fabric or woven fabric might require machine stitching (straight, zig-zag, or overlock) along the raw edge to prevent raveling. Be careful not to stretch the raw edge as you're stitching.

⌇. BRAID OR RIBBON EDGING

Trimming sweaters with purchased braids or ribbons can solve that "This-sweater-needs-something" dilemma in a snap. Buy trim that can be laundered with your sweater fabric. Some ribbons and braids are labeled "dry clean only" and might shrink, fade, or fall apart if washed.

To avoid any incompatibility in cleaning, match trim and fabric fiber for fiber, that is, polyester to polyester, acrylic to acrylic, etc. (This fiber matching makes color matching easier too.) Trims should always be pre-laundered the same way as you would the finished garment.

Braid or ribbon edging is ideal for cardigans and placket front closures. Machine buttonholes are easily made on these trims and the trim stabilizes the edges. Toggle closures also work well.

Although the number of knit trims available on the market is increasing, most decorative braids and ribbons are woven. These nonstretch woven trims restrict the stretchability of any sweater edge where they're applied. So don't sew woven or limited-stretch trims to fitted necklines, cuffs, waistlines, etc., or you'll make a beautiful garment that can't be put on.

APPLYING FLAT BRAIDS AND RIBBONS

1. Shape the trim to the neckline, armhole, or cuff curves with your steam iron.
   - It's difficult to shape a tightly woven trim to extreme convex or concave curves. In this case, angle or "square" the corners.
   - On V or square corners miter the trim to fit (see page 56).

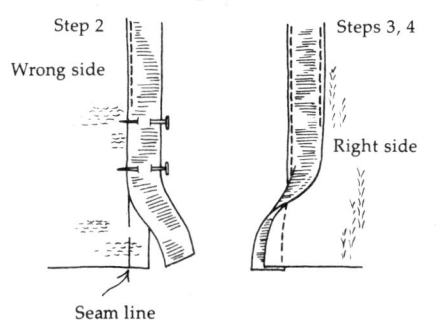

2. Place the trim on the wrong side of the sweater fabric, aligning the finished trim edge on the designated seam line (wrong sides together). Straight stitch by machine (8 stitches per inch) close to the trim edge over the seam line.

3. Turn trim to the right side of garment. Align the stitched trim edge over the fold. Steam press lightly.

4. Topstitch the trim in place close to the other edge. All raw seam edges will be enclosed.

MITERING FLAT BRAIDS AND RIBBONS

Use the following technique to form inside and outside corners. The steps for either are the same but the illustrations clarify the different look of each kind of corner. Use these corners on necklines, armscye, pockets, plackets, cuffs, and side vents.

1. Stitch the trim on the wrong side of the fabric as previously instructed for flat braids and ribbons, up to the seam line pivot point. Back stitch. Leave a 2" trim extension and cut the trim.

2. Allowing for another 2" trim extension, stitch a piece of trim from the seam line pivot point. Backstitch for reinforcement.

3. Clip away outside corner fabric. Slash to pivot point on inside corner.

4. Miter the corner by stitching across the diagonal seam. Trim seam allowances.

5. Topstitch the trim in place, close to the other trim edge.

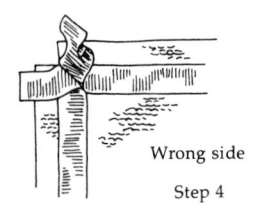

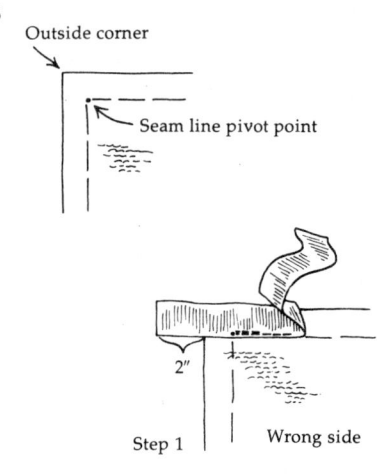

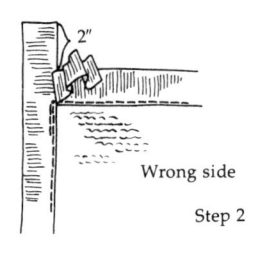

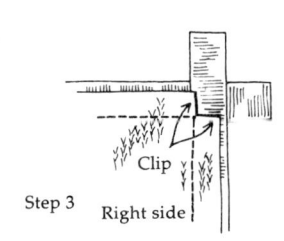

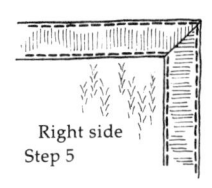

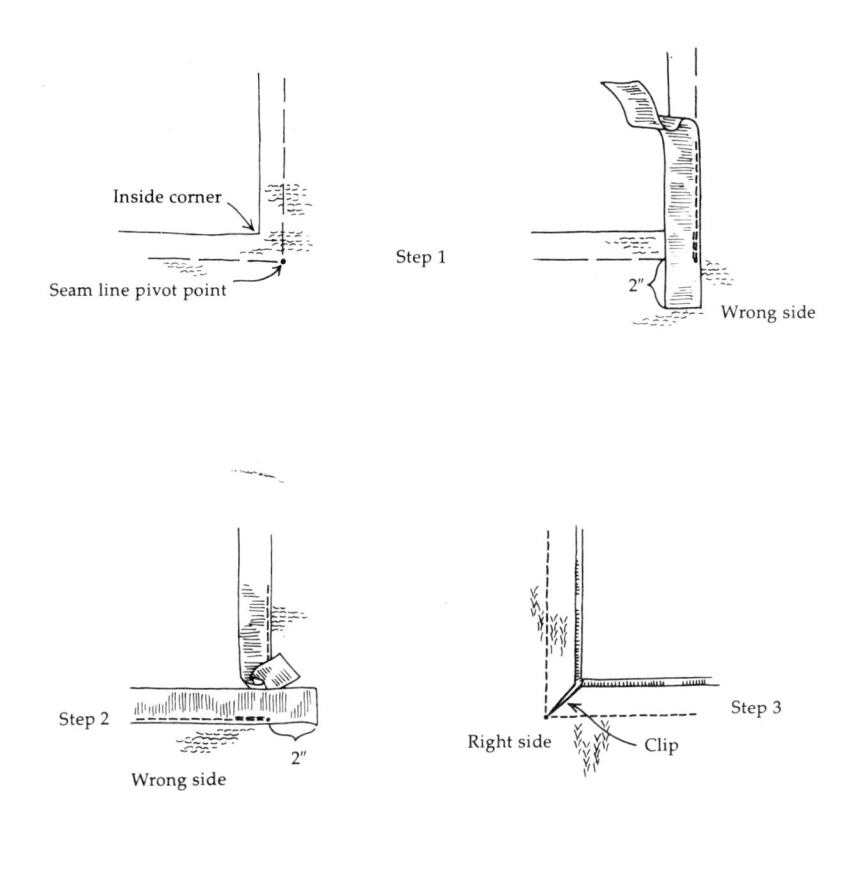

Sweater Sewing • 61

Inside corner
Seam line pivot point
Step 1

2"
Wrong side

Step 2
Wrong side
2"

Right side
Clip
Step 3

Step 4 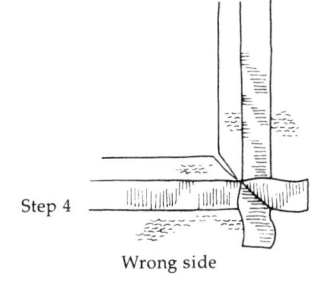
Wrong side

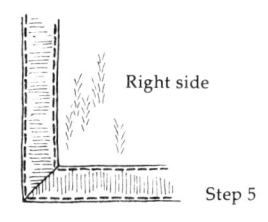

Right side
Step 5

TRIM APPLICATION FOR A FINISHED EDGE

• Since hand-knitted or crocheted garments have finished sweater fabric edges, trim can just be topstitched on without seaming. Shape to fit curves and angles. Miter corners and angles using the technique on page 56.

• Use decorative machine stitches to apply trim to sweater fabric.

• Bulkier trims like hand crochet, braid, or macrame can be sewn on by hand. Since they are difficult to shape and miter, use for straight or just slightly curved edges.

✄. CASINGS FOR ELASTIC

Since most people want to minimize their waistlines, elastic-cased waistbands should be as flat and smooth fitting as possible, and they'll be more comfortable too. Elastic casings can also be used to finish sleeve cuffs and jacket hems.

Buy 1"–1½" washable nonroll elastic. This type won't turn and twist during washing and wearing.

To determine the correct length, place the elastic around your waist until it's comfortably snug. Add 1" to the length for seam allowances (½" overlap on each end). To allow for the bulk of heavy sweater fabrics, add an extra inch to the length of the elastic.

CASING FOR SWEATER FABRIC BY THE YARD

1. Before you cut out the pattern, add fabric equal to two times the width of the elastic plus one seam allowance for the casing.
2. Fit the 1"–1½" elastic to the body area, i.e., waist, cuff, etc. Lap the elastic, then stitch to form a circle.
3. Fold the casing toward the wrong side of the fabric. Place the elastic inside the fold edge.
4. Straight stitch to enclose the elastic inside the casing. Don't catch the elastic in the stitching.
5. Try on the garment. Distribute the ease for the most flattering, comfortable fit. Then stitch in the ditch (see page 57) in any casing seam to hold the elastic and ease in place.

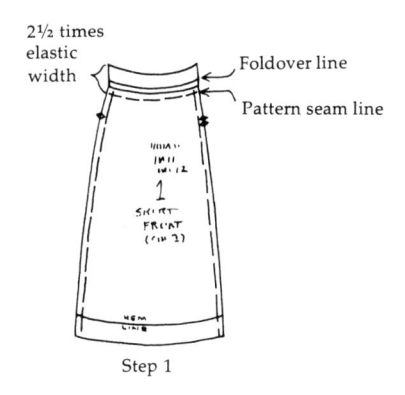

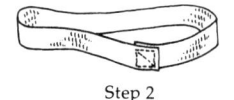

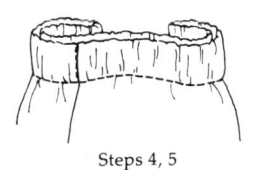

Step 1

Step 2

Steps 4, 5

CASING FOR SWEATER BODIES

The sweater body's finished rib edge (which should not be less than 2" long for this technique) serves as the elastic casing, eliminating seaming and bulk.

1. Use ¾"–1" elastic. Lap, and stitch to form a circle.
2. Fold the ribbed edge in half toward the wrong side over the elastic.
3. Set your machine on a straight, zig-zag, or stretch stitch. Stitch along the finished rib edge, making the casing for the elastic. Don't catch the elastic in the stitching.
- For sweaters that must withstand rough wear, stitch again next to previous row to keep the elastic from popping out.
4. Stitch in the ditch (see page 57) in casing seams to hold the elastic and fabric ease in place.

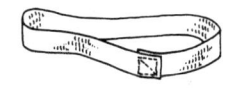

Step 1

If the sweater body has a narrow ribbed edge, or is very bulky, try the following technique.

1. Fit the elastic very snugly to the body area, stretching elastic slightly. Lap the elastic and stitch to form a circle.

2. Place the elastic 1/8"–1/4" from the finished rib edge on the wrong side of the fabric. Distribute the fabric ease evenly on the elastic, then pin.

3. Set your machine on a stretch or zig-zag stitch. Stitch over the elastic on both long edges, to hold the elastic in place.

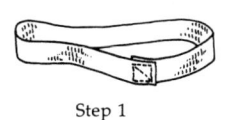

Step 1

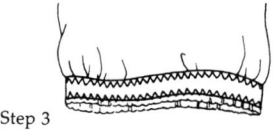

Step 3

CASING FOR HAND-KNITTED OR CROCHETED SWEATERS

Because most hand-knitted or crocheted sweater fabrics are bulkier than machine-mades, you should avoid making conventional elastic casings for them. Here's how to get around the problem.

1. Fit the elastic, lap, and stitch to form a circle. Finish off the sweater fabric to the desired length (no casing is necessary).

2. Thread a yarn needle with a single strand of matching yarn. Apply the elastic by hand with a large catch stitch just inside the fabric edge (see page 77).

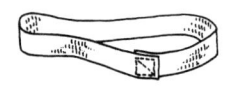

The elastic controls the ease, without adding casing bulk. Be careful when you pull these garments on and off because the large catch stitch can be easily snagged.

Step 1

NECKLINE FINISHES

Sweaters get their names from their necklines—crewnecks, boatnecks, turtlenecks. Take care in finishing this very important element to ensure a professional look for your project.

CREWNECK, BOATNECK, MOCK TURTLE, AND TURTLENECK SWEATERS

These classic sweater styles call for edge control around the neckline area. Cut the ribbing just large enough to fit the head size when stretched and hug the neck when relaxed.

Before choosing one of these neckline finishes, test the ribbing for stretch and recovery. Ribbings that stretch excessively result in "growing necklines." After being pulled on and off a few times, a turtleneck could grow into a cowl style!

1. Measure the height of the neckline finish. Don't forget to allow for double thicknesses and fold-over turtlenecks. To determine ribbing circumference, stretch ribbing around your head snugly. Add ⅝" seam allowance.

Step 1

2. Straight stitch the ribbing, right sides together on the ⅝" seam line. Press open. Fold ribbing in half, right side out.

3. Divide the neckline ribbing into quarter sections. Divide the neck edge of the sweater into quarters. Mark with pins.

4. Place ribbing and sweater right sides together matching pins. *Note:* The shoulder seams will not usually fall at the quarter marks.

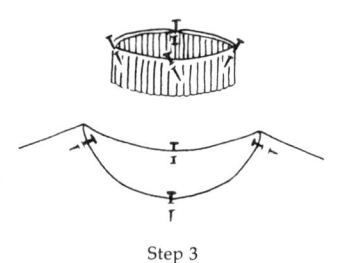

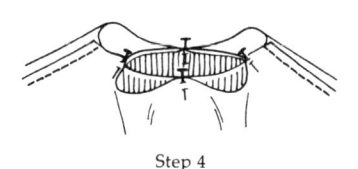

Step 3

Step 4

(*Note:* pins are not at shoulder seams)

With the ribbing on top next to the presser foot, stitch with a sweater seam (see page 53). Stretch the ribbing to fit each quarter section using ease plus (see page 52). *Note:* If you don't have an overlock stitch use any sweater seam technique (see page 53).

5. Necklines stand straighter on crew and mock turtle styles if you topstitch ¼" from the shoulder and back neckline seams, catching all inside seams.

Step 5

Center back

TIGHT, TALL TURTLENECKS

Supertight fitting, tall turtlenecks are sure-fire fashion, but if bulky they look like neck braces and can be uncomfortable too.

Ready-to-wear manufacturers have solved this problem by cutting out the turtleneck piece single layer, twice the desired height, plus ½" hem and ⅝" seam allowances. If turtleneck edges are not finished, turn under ½" and stitch with a straight stitch or an elastic machine stitch such as a multiple zig-zag.

Determine the turtleneck ribbing circumference by stretching it to fit your head *very* snugly.

1. Starting from the raw edge, sew the turtleneck band wrong sides together to the fold line. Backstitch and clip to stitch line. Trim excess seam allowance. This seam will lie against the neck.

2. Starting from the finished hem edge, right sides together, stitch toward the fold line. This seam will be hidden inside the turtleneck.

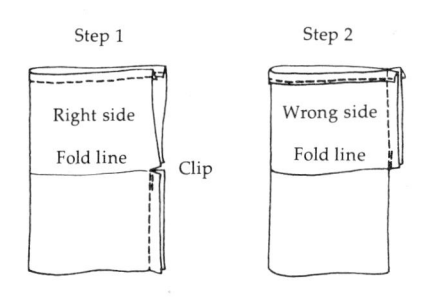

Step 1
Right side
Fold line
Clip

Step 2
Wrong side
Fold line

3. Turn down along the fold line.
Follow Steps 1, 3, 4, 5 for Crewneck, Boatneck, Mock Turtle, and Turtleneck Sweaters (see page 64).

↙. V-NECK SWEATERS

V necklines are big on the sweater scene for men, women, and children. But nothing shouts "homemade" more loudly than a crooked, poorly fitting, or stretched-out V neckline. Here's a mistake-proof method for a professional V every time!

Ribbing, binding, and trim should hug the nape of the neck. To create a smooth-fitting back neckline, use ribbing two thirds the size of the back neck curve measurement (2" of ribbing to 3" of back neckline curve). If you're using a very stable ribbing/trim or self-fabric, measure it 1/2"–1" smaller than the back neck edge.

MITERED V

1. Pin mark the amount of ribbing/trim needed.
2. Match to shoulder seams and measure front V neckline on both sides. Mark center front on ribbing/trim band with pins and allow for 1½" seam allowances at both ends. Your fitted ribbing/trim is ready to apply!
3. Match pins to shoulder seams and center front, stretching ribbing/trim to the neckline contour.

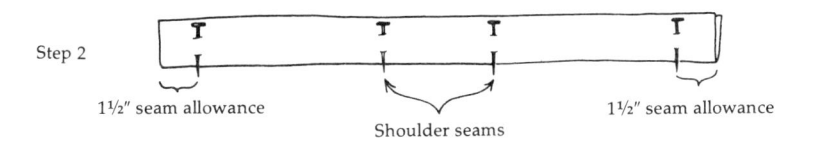

Step 2

1½" seam allowance — Shoulder seams — 1½" seam allowance

4. Stitch to center back from each side of the V. Make sure you start stitching exactly on the center front line. Reinforce V with backstitching. The two stitching lines should form an even V for a professional finish.

5. With sharp scissors clip down to the point of the V.

6. Align a ruler along the sweater center front line and mark the front ribbing/trim seam line. Pin baste along this marked seam line.

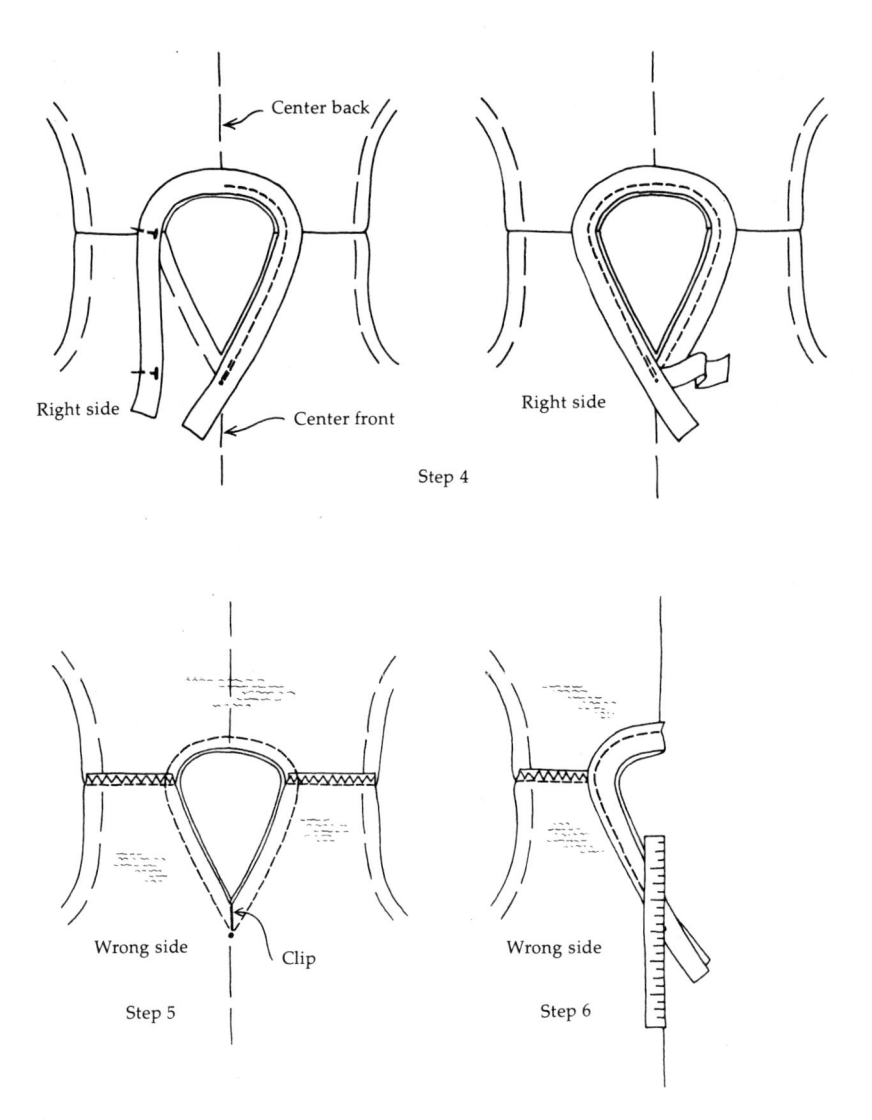

Step 4

Step 5

Step 6

Sweater Sewing • 69

7. Next, try on the sweater, right side out. Look in a mirror. Is the miter centered? (The human figure is rarely symmetrical.) If not, make necessary adjustments.

8. Stitch along the seam line. Open the mitered seam and tack down to ribbing/trim by hand or machine.

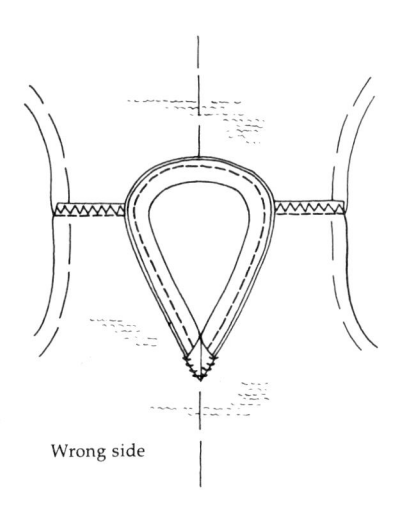

Seam line

Wrong side

Step 8

Wrong side

LAPPED V

Follow Steps 1, 2, 3 for the Mitered V.

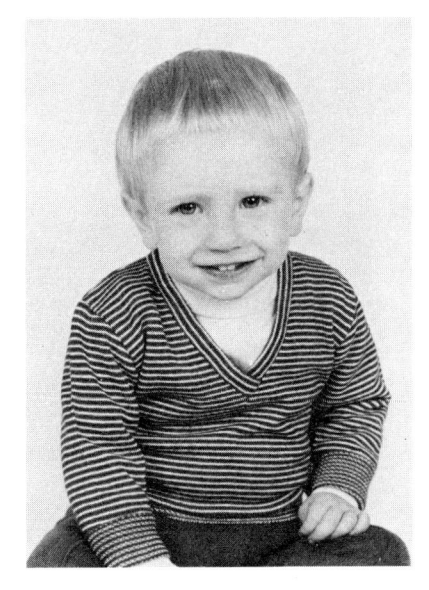

4. Start the left side stitching line 2" above the V point. (Women's sweaters lap right over left, men's left over right.) Stitch to center back.

5. Reinforce the 2" space with stay stitching along the seam line to the V point.

6. On the right side, stitch the ribbing/trim from the V point (center front) to the center back.

7. Clip to the V point.

8. Lap the right trim extension over the unsewn left trim extension. Fold under the unsewn 2" seam allowance along the stay stitching line.

9. Adjust the ribbing/trim so that the V is even and flat. Try on the sweater to make sure the lapped V is centered and not puckered.

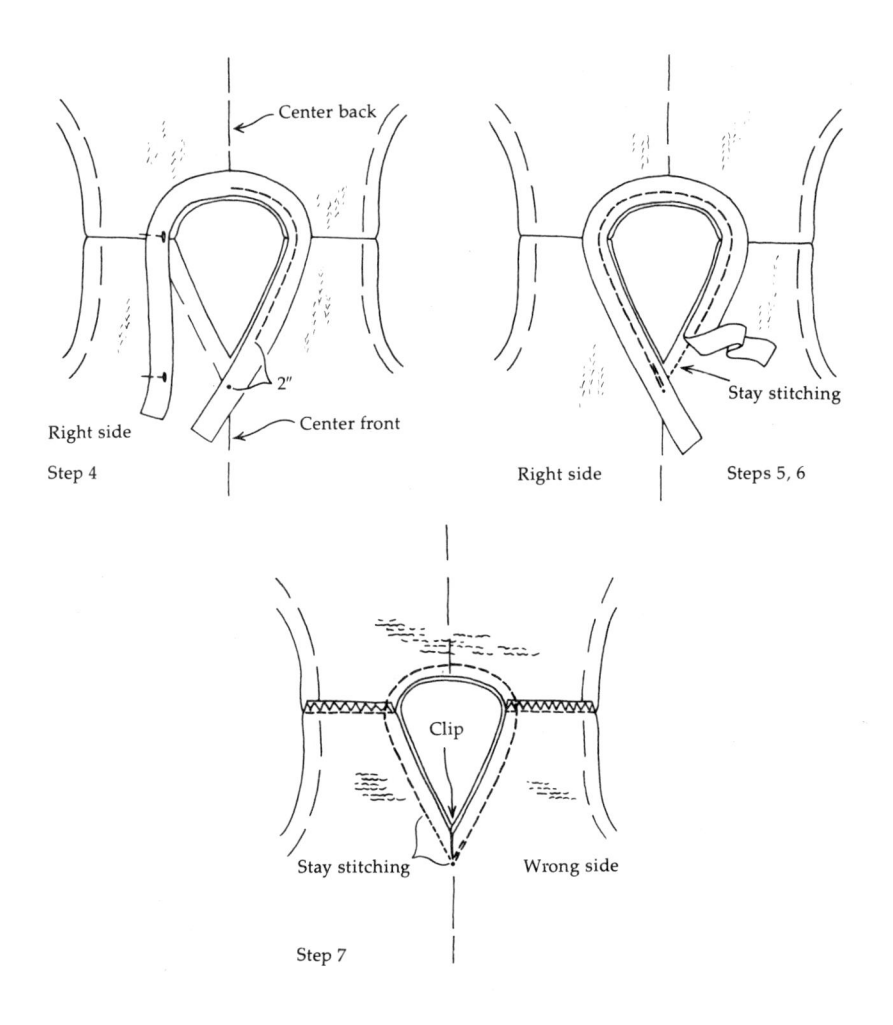

Right side

Step 4

Right side

Steps 5, 6

Step 7

10. Sew the lap in place from the wrong side, ribbing/trim next to the foot. Stitch through the sweater seam allowance and the two trim strips. This stitching should start exactly on the V point. The ribbing/trim should be an even width to the V point.

11. Trim the extensions to the seam stitching. Tack the lap extension to the seam by hand or machine.

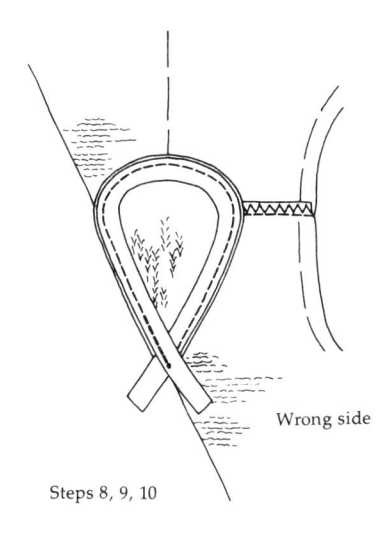

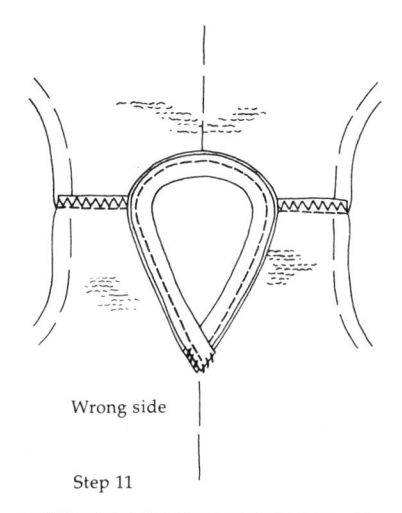

Steps 8, 9, 10

Step 11

✄. CARDIGAN SWEATERS

The cardigan is a stylish, classic sweater that flatters everyone—men, women, and children. There are several ways to finish the neckline. It can join into the front edge and go down to the hem with the use of ribbing, binding, ribbon, or trim. Or, the neckline can be a length of ribbing, the front edge stabilized with grosgrain ribbon and closed with buttons or toggles. The cardigan is a versatile component of a sweater wardrobe.

CARDIGAN WITH RIBBED NECKLINE AND FRONT EDGE

1. Stitch the shoulder seams.
2. Hem if you are not using a prefinished sweater body.
3. Pin ribbing in place. Stitch from the center back and down one side to the hem for even distribution of ease. Repeat on the other side.
4. Turn the ribbing to the wrong side and tack with hand stitches.

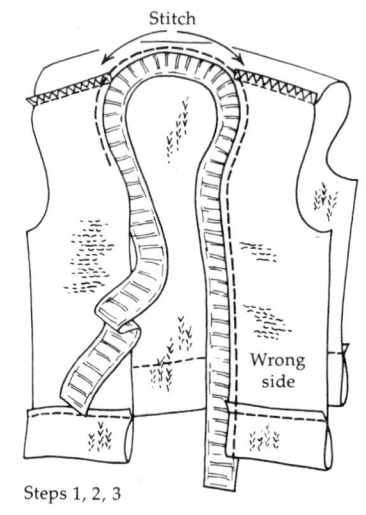

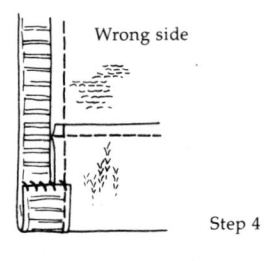

Steps 1, 2, 3

Step 4

STABILIZING EDGES WITH GROSGRAIN RIBBON

You can use grosgrain ribbon (usually 1" wide) to finish front edges of sweaters, invisibly! Finishing with grosgrain ribbon stabilizes sweater buttonholes too. If you're finishing a washable sweater knit fabric, use 100 percent polyester grosgrain ribbon. Pre-wash all ribbons before sewing.

1. Finish neck edge with ribbing.
   - See Ribbing—the All-Purpose Edging, page 55.
2. Cut ribbon the length of the front opening plus 2". Measure the pattern, not the sweater.

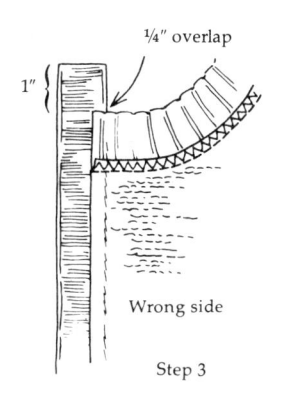

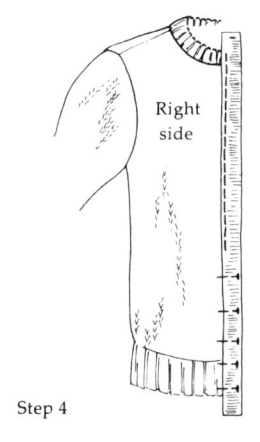

3. Pin ribbon on the right side of the sweater along a ¼" overlap, leaving 1" at the top and 1" at the bottom. Ease the front edge of the sweater to the grosgrain ribbon. Pin in place.

4. Straight stitch close to the grosgrain ribbon edge to prevent stretching. For even distribution of ease, stitch from the ribbon side of the seam.

5. Turn the ribbon to the inside of the sweater and press. Fold under ends of ribbon and hand stitch in place. *Note:* When facing with ribbon on two edges at right angles, miter inside corner to eliminate bulk (see page 56).

6. Work buttonholes. Top buttonholes on the neckband or ribbing of most cardigans are horizontal. The other buttonholes are vertical. Position buttonholes and buttons in the middle of the grosgrain ribbon. (For men's and boys' sweaters, buttonholes go on the left; for women's and girls', the right.)

The free edge of the grosgrain ribbon doesn't need to be stitched down because the buttonholes and buttons hold the ribbon in place.

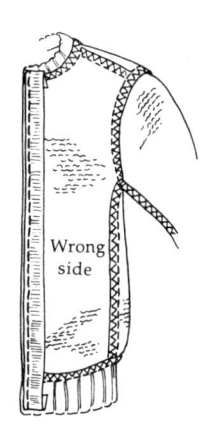

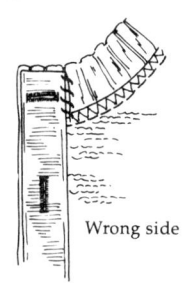

HEMS AND CUFFS

A stretched-out or too-visible hem makes a sweater look homemade too. Some experimentation may be required to determine the best technique for your fabric. Sweater hems and sleeve hems are really very simple and quick to do, if you choose the appropriate technique for the style and fabric. Remember, sweater hems should give. Machine or hand stitches that restrict the elasticity of the hem cause fitting problems and eventually break during wear.

➤ HEM BEFORE SEWING SEAMS?

Look at some of your ready-to-wear sweaters. You'll notice that most sweaters were *hemmed before they were seamed.* This technique not only streamlines the manufacturing process, but it also helps solve the hem-stretch problem.

When more controllable, smaller sections of the sweater garment are hemmed separately, there is less tendency to pull the hem edge out of shape. It's also easier to hem when the garment is flat, especially on tight-fitting sleeves.

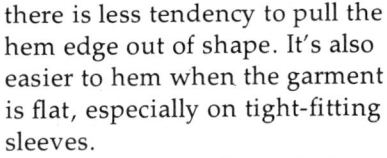

In order to use this technique you must predetermine the position of the hem either by length measurements or by trying on the pinned-together pattern.

1. Straight stitch the seam from the hem up, matching the hem edges.
2. Along hem edges, turn in the seam edge corners toward the seam line.
3. Stitch seam again (see page 53). Trim close to second stitching.

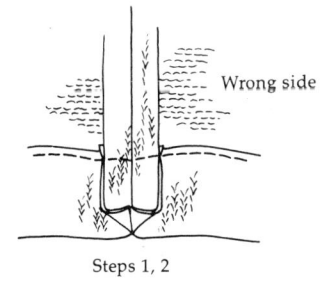

Wrong side

Steps 1, 2

➤ MACHINE-STITCHED TURN-UP HEMS

Keep the hem depth in sweater knits as small as possible, not larger than 2". The larger the flare of any sweater garment, the smaller the hem should be. A smaller hem is lighter and bouncier.

When you hem by machine, always test the selected hemming technique on a sample swatch of sweater fabric. If stretching of the hem edge is a problem, try lightening the foot pressure (see page 47) or using the ease plus technique (see page 52).

If you have sewn standard seams, avoid bulk by trimming seam allowances to ⅜" starting at bottom edge and ending at hem fold line.

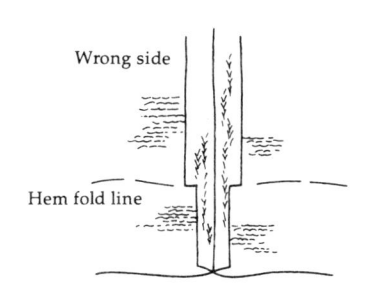

BLIND STITCHED HEMS

On most zig-zag and stretch stitch machine models, there is a blind stitch setting. This flexible stitch is a great hemming tool for bulkier sweater knits because it hides the stitches in the fabric texture or design.

To stabilize the edge you can ease plus straight stitch ¼" from the raw edge before following these steps.

1. Turn up the hem to the desired length (hem depth not more than 2"). With the wrong side up, fold the garment back so that the fold is ¼" from the raw edge.

2. Blind stitch so that the straight stitching lands about ¼" from the raw edge and the zig-zag barely catches the garment fold.

• If the zig-zag catches too much of the sweater, it causes puckering and the hem will show through on the right side. Either re-position the blind stitch or make the zig-zag narrower.

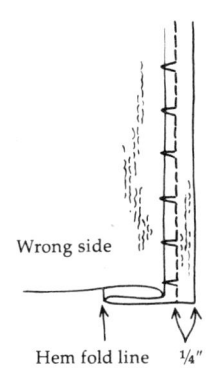

TOPSTITCHED HEMS

The fastest way to hem sweaters! Just turn up the hem, steam press, and stitch. Stitching can be any distance from the folded edge, although ½"–1" is standard. Set stitch length at 6–8 stitches per inch.

Double topstitching stabilizes

hems (and neckline edges) and is decorative too.

Space the topstitching at equal intervals from the hem fold. Stitch with the right side of the sweater up. Be careful not to stretch the hem while stitching.

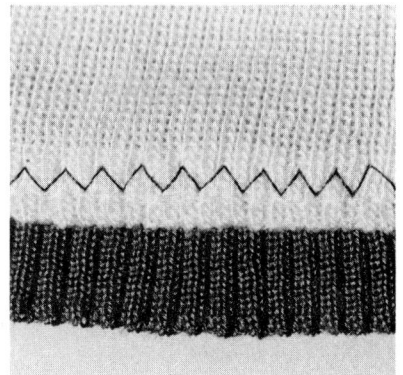

MACHINE-FLOUNCED HEMS

On the lightest of sweater knits machine flouncing adds a ruffled effect to hems, collars, and cuffs.

Turn up the hem ¼" on the wrong side of the garment. On the right side of the fabric zigzag stitch next to the hem fold. Stretch the edge as you stitch. The more the edge is stretched, the curlier the flounce will be.

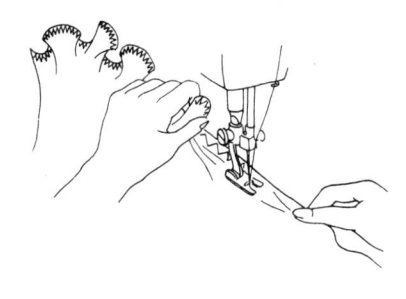

⨽. HAND-STITCHED HEMS

It's not very effective to finish the raw hem edge of a sweater as you would ravel-prone woven fabrics, since seam bindings, laces, zig-zagging, or clean finishing the hem edge create unsightly ridges on the right side of the sweater. The following method saves time and money, and eliminates bulk.

When you hand stitch hems, keep stitches as loose as possible so they give with the sweater and do not show on the right side. Make *very tiny* stitches in the garment itself.

CATCH STITCH

A very elastic stitch that's recommended for most hand-stitched sweater hems is the catch stitch.

1. Ease plus straight stitch ¼" from the raw edge to prepare the hem edge (see page 52). If the fabric is knitted very loosely, hand overcast the raw edge to prevent raveling.

2. Pin the hem in place. Fold down the hem along the ¼" stitching line. Work from left to right (right to left for lefties) and catch the garment and hem with loose stitches.

On sweater knits that are very lightweight or loosely knitted, you can work the catch stitch over the raw hem edge. If the stitches are loose enough, this hem technique does not show on the right side of the sweater.

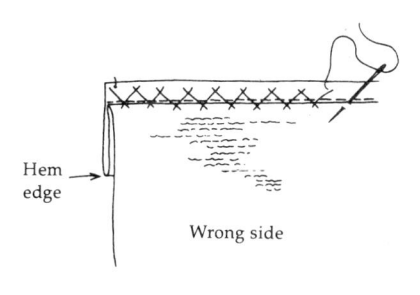

Step 2

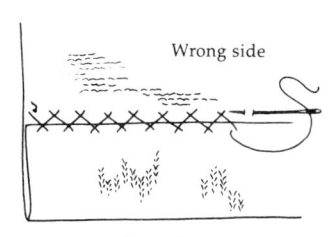

Lightweight knits

78 • THE SUPER SWEATER IDEA BOOK

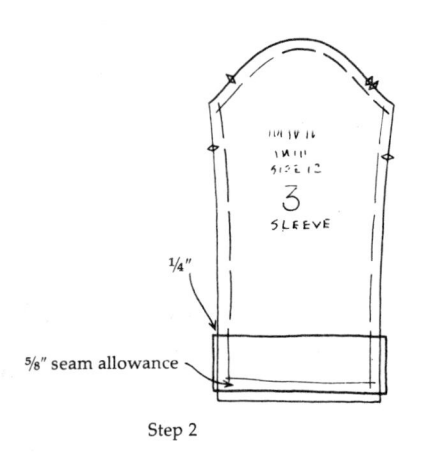

⌒. CUFFS

On sweater sleeves you can add cuffs instead of a hem. Cuffs are also great for heavy jackets and coats.

1. Decide upon the depth and thickness (double or single layer) of the cuff.

2. Draw the cuff pattern. Trace from the sleeve pattern, as shown, allowing an extra ¼" on each seam and ⅝" along the bottom edge. Don't make the cuffs too tight or floppy. If the cuffs are to be double thickness, don't forget to double the depth.

3. Cut the cuffs from self-fabric, bias wovens, or contrasting color sweater knit.

4. Sew the cuff seam, right sides together. Press open the seam.

• If cuffs are double thickness, fold along the fold line with wrong sides together. Sew cuff seam.

5. Stitch the sweater sleeve, right sides together. Trim the excess seam allowance.

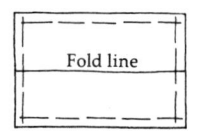

Step 2

Double thickness cuff

6. Stitch the cuff to the sleeve hem raw edge, right side of the cuff to wrong side of the sweater matching cuff and sleeve seams and distributing the ½" cuff ease evenly across the sleeve.

7. Double stitch the seam (see Sweater Seams, page 53). Trim. Turn the cuff to the right side of the sleeve. The joining seam is hidden inside the cuff!

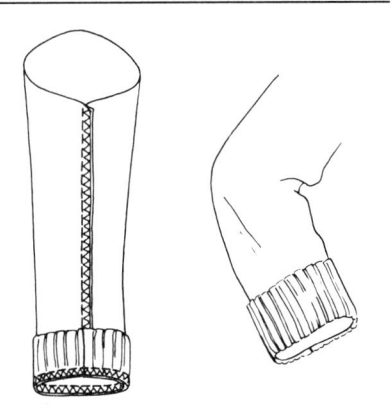

SWEATER CLOSURES

There is a wide choice of closures that can be applied to the very versatile sweater—buttons, zippers, toggles. Refer to Chapter 4, Sweater Design Workshop, for additional closure ideas.

NO-STRETCH BUTTONHOLES

Stretched-out buttonholes can ruin the custom look of any sweater. With no-stretch buttonholes you can eliminate "fish mouth" buttonholes once and for all!

Try this designer's tip for tight-lipped machine buttonholes every time.

1. Follow your sewing machine manual to prepare the machine for sewing buttonholes. Set the machine at 10–12 stitches per inch. (Too many stitches per inch results in stretched, bulky buttonholes.) Stitch over buttonhole twist or crochet or embroidery thread, leaving a loop on the end.

2. When buttonhole is completed, pull the loose cording end, hiding the cord loop beneath the bar tack (see Step 8, page 86). With a needle bring the loose cord ends to the back side, tie, and clip.

- Reinforcing buttonhole areas with fusible interfacings can solve the "fish-mouth" problem. Steam fuse a small piece of the interfacing to the back of the buttonhole area. The interfacing will be hidden in the buttonhole stitching. *Note:* Always test fusibles on a sample swatch of fabric before ironing onto the garment.
- Another sweater secret: Stitch buttonholes vertically instead of horizontally to minimize stretch.
- For a handmade look, stitch by hand over machine stitching with lightweight yarn and a small, even blanket stitch (see page 118).

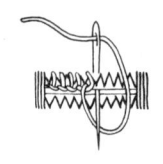

- When you're sewing heavy gauge or very stretchable sweater knits, avoid buttonhole styles; wrapped or pullover patterns are more workable. When necessary, hand work buttonholes with yarn or thread on these knits (see Blanket Stitch, page 118).

ZIPPERS

Because sweaters are stretchable, zippers are seldom used as closures. But many polo sweaters have exposed neckline zippers and certain jacket styles have front separating zippers. Some people like zippers in everything to avoid pulling garments over their hairdos and makeup.

Nylon or polyester zippers are better than metal types because they're light and flexible. If it's difficult to find separating zippers in nylon and polyester, buy the lightest metal type you can find.

You can sew in zippers by hand or by machine. Hand-sewn applications are suggested for very stretchy, fuzzy, lacy, or bulky fabrics. For either application technique, it's important not to let the fabric edge get stretched out of shape. If the edge is stretched out, the zipper won't lie flat.

The following installation methods are specially designed for sweater zippers. You can sew all of them in by hand or machine. If you sew in a zipper by machine, be sure to use a zipper foot. If you sew by hand, use a small backstitch and matching double-strand thread.

CENTERED DOUBLE-LAP APPLICATION OF NON-SEPARATING ZIPPER

1. Sew the seam up to the zipper opening. Fold under the seam allowance the length of the zipper opening.

2. To stabilize the edge, sew a ¼" pre-shrunk twill tape in the seam allowance fold.

3. For reinforcement and decoration, blanket stitch around the zipper opening before sewing in the zipper. The blanket stitches guide the zipper installation.

4. Close zipper and align the zipper teeth under the folded edges. When zipper is closed the folded edges should meet, hiding the zipper.

5. Baste the zipper in the opening. Don't use pins because they might cause crooked sewing.

6. Sew the zipper in, by hand or machine, approximately ⅜" from the seam line. Square off the bottom.

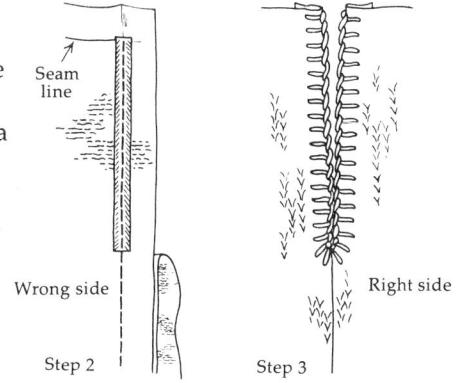

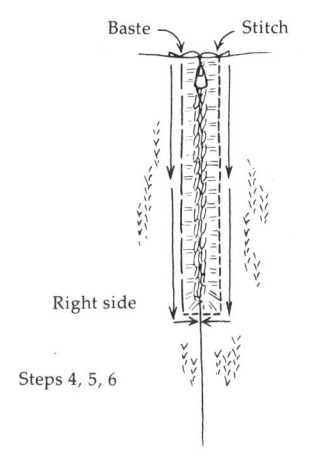

- On very stretchable knits or on matching stripes, stitch directionally, from top to bottom (or bottom to top) on both sides of the zipper. Do not stretch the opening edge as you're sewing.

DOUBLE-LAP APPLICATION OF SEPARATING ZIPPER

1. Baste along the designated seam lines, using the ease plus technique to prevent stretching (see page 52).

2. To further stabilize the zipper opening, sew a ¼" preshrunk twill tape along the stitching lines on the wrong side.

3. Fold under the seam allowance. Baste in the zipper, hiding the teeth under the folded edges.

4. Sew in the zipper, directionally, approximately ⅜" from the folded edge. Then finish with a backstitch.

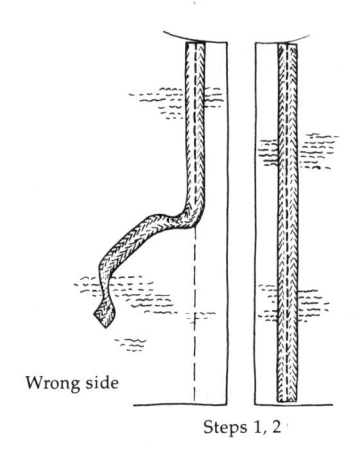

Wrong side

Steps 1, 2

Right side

Steps 3, 4

EXPOSED SEPARATING ZIPPERS

Use this method for decorative zippers with big teeth seen in so many sporty sweaters and warm-up jackets.

1. Baste along the designated seam line, as per instructions for the double-lap application of separating zipper. Place this stitching line close to the zipper teeth with the right side of the fabric next to the right side of the zipper.

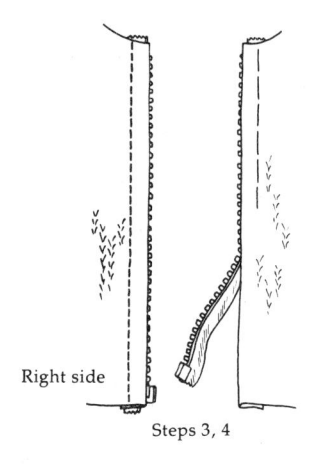

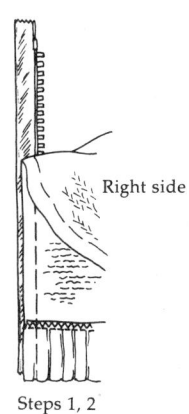

Right side

Steps 1, 2

2. Baste the zipper in place, being careful not to stretch the folded edges.

3. Stitch from the wrong side of the fabric, along the seam line, next to the zipper teeth. Backstitch at both open ends.

4. For decoration and to hold the zipper tape in place, topstitch ¼"–⅜" from the teeth, using a long straight stitch (6–8 stitches per inch).

- Do not pull the fabric off grain while topstitching.

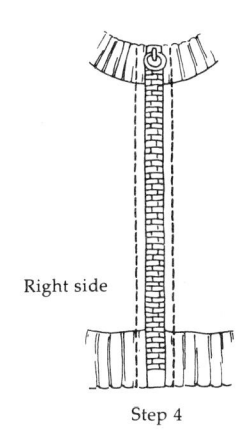

Right side

Step 4

EXPOSED NON-SEPARATING ZIPPER: HANDMADES

On some handmade sweater fabrics with finished-edge zipper openings, you can sew in the zipper by hand without turning under seam allowances. An exposed application is particularly suitable for handmades that are extra bulky and fuzzy. Sew in the zipper with a backstitch and matching thread or yarn.

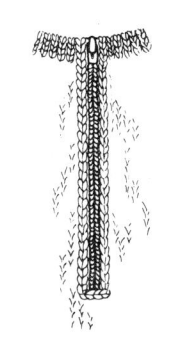

EXPOSED NON-SEPARATING ZIPPER: CUT-AND-SEWNS

Cut-and-sewn sweaters do not have finished edges along the zipper openings. For these sweaters the zipper application is sewn in a slash rather than a seam. Finish the neckline edge before installing the zipper.

1. Mark the zipper opening with a line of machine basting the length of the zipper.

2. Stay stitch ¼" on either side of this basting line, using the ease plus technique to prevent stretching (see page 52). Square off the bottom.

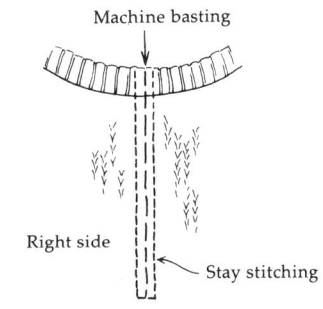

Machine basting

Right side

Stay stitching

3. Place the closed zipper upside down on the right side of the fabric, positioning the bottom zipper stop just below the stay stitching line.

4. Stitch across the zipper tape the width of the stay stitching.

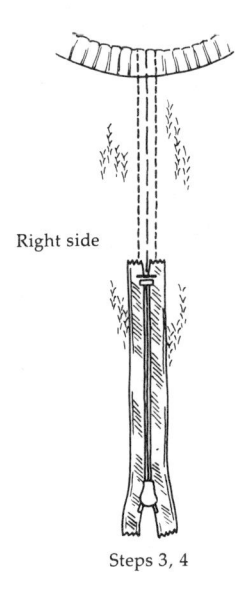

5. Starting at the neckline edge, cut along the basting line to the bottom stay stitching line. Turn the zipper up to the neckline edge.

6. Working with one side of the zipper at a time, place the stay stitching line next to the zipper teeth. Stitch over the stay stitching line from top to bottom. Backstitch. Repeat on the other side.

7. To finish the neckline edge, turn down the zipper tape and whipstitch in place.

Right side

Steps 3, 4

Right side

Step 5

Wrong side

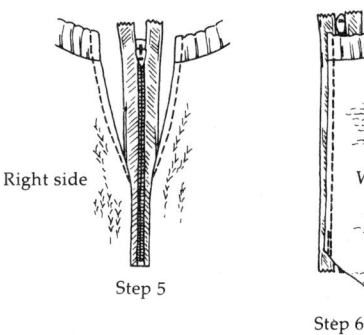

Step 6

BOUND-EDGE SEPARATING ZIPPER

1. Trim off the zipper opening seam allowances.

2. Cut 2" bias strips from woven fabric. Stitch the bias strip to the zipper opening, right sides together, with a ⅜" seam.

3. Fold the bias back to form a ⅜" finished binding trim.

4. Insert the zipper and stitch in the ditch, around the binding edge, aligning the zipper teeth with the edge (see page 57).

INVISIBLY STITCHED SWEATER POCKETS

Pockets are practically an indispensable fashion addition to any sweater. You can sew on patch pockets invisibly and quickly with the following technique specially designed for stretch fabrics.

1. Prepare top edge of pocket. Apply ribbing or trim, or hem the pocket by machine or hand. Or cut out the pocket double along a fold line, and fold along the top edge line, wrong sides together.

2. Straight stitch around the pocket ½" from the raw edge with the machine set on 8–10 stitches to the inch.

3. Set the machine on the longest basting stitch. Stitch around the pocket again, ¼" from the raw edge.

4. Pull the basting thread so that the seam allowance folds toward the wrong side of the pocket. The basting thread controls the fullness on pocket curves.

5. Pin the pocket to the garment just inside the pocket markings, wrong side of the pocket to right side of the sweater. Place the right side up and use the longest and narrowest zig-zag stitch to machine baste the pocket in place very close to the pocket edge.

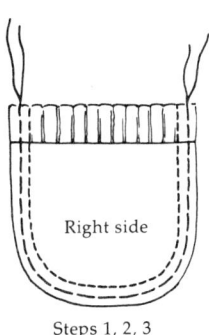

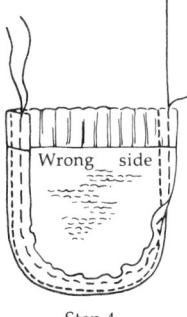

Steps 1, 2, 3

Step 4

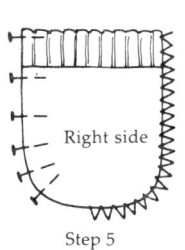

Step 5

Step 6

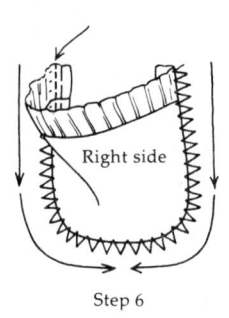

- For very stretchable or bulky sweaters, catch stitch the pocket in place by hand.

6. On the inside of the pocket, straight stitch directly over the first ½" stitching line. (Yes! You can actually get the presser foot inside the pocket because of the sweater stretch!) Stitch from each top edge of the pocket to the center bottom.

7. Remove basting. Trim pocket seam allowances to minimize bulk.

8. To reinforce top pocket corners, blindstitch ¼"–½" along the top edge or make triangular bar tacks. To make a bar tack, straight stitch or zig-zag the outline of a triangle that measures ¼" across the top and ⅝" down the sides.

CHAPTER 4

SWEATER DESIGN WORKSHOP

Your basic sweater pattern can be the blueprint for a wardrobe of designer originals of your own! Sweaters have such simple lines that by varying just the fabric, sleeve, neckline, trim, or closure you can create an all-new look. With the ideas given in this chapter, you can transform the basic sweater pattern with stripes, toggles, crocheted edging, or smocking. Use your imagination. It's fun, and the sweater design possibilities are simply endless!

SIGNATURED SWEATER CRAFT GARMENTS

Put your personal signature on any sweater craft project with initial monograms. Signature sweater pockets—even corners of afghans or pillows. You'll make sweater craft gifts all-their-own with these monogram methods.

✂. APPLIQUÉ MONOGRAMS

A very simple monogram method uses purchased appliqué initials. Pre-wash appliqués to prevent color running or shrinkage. Sew the initials on by hand or by machine with a straight or zig-zag stitch. Machine application is easier on a pocket *before* it is sewn to the sweater. If the letters slip while you're stitching, cellophane tape them in place (don't use pins because they're difficult to sew over). After stitching is completed, remove the tape.

✂. TRIM OR BRAID MONOGRAMS

Monograms can also be made from tapes, trims, or braids. Always pre-wash, then form into the shape of the initials. Miter square corners (see page 56). Attach with pins or cellophane tape. Stitch the initial design in place, using a narrow zig-zag or straight stitch (6–8 stitches per inch).

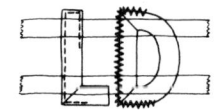

✂. YARN MONOGRAMS

You can also form initial monograms with yarn. A zig-zag machine is necessary for this method. Test stitch on a sample swatch.

1. Draw or trace the monogram letters on tracing paper. To make sewing easier, the design of the initials should be continuous (script), rather than broken (block print style). Pin or tape the tracing paper pattern in place on the sweater.
2. Straight stitch, following the monogram lines, through the sweater fabric (6–8 stitches per inch). Then tear off the paper.
3. Allowing a 2″–3″ extension at the beginning and at the end,

guide the yarn along the contour of the monogram. Sew over the yarn with a zig-zag stitch set to land on both sides of the yarn.

4. Draw both yarn extensions and all thread ends through to the wrong side of the fabric and fasten back into the zig-zag stitch.

Try this method for freehand designs too.

HANDCRAFTED DECORATIVE SEAMS

If you're away from your sewing machine—watching television, traveling, or on vacation—seam sweater craft garments together by hand. Handmade seams are portable.

You can crochet or sew seams together with yarn. For either method use yarn of similar or lighter weight than the sweater fabric to prevent bulk. Crocheting produces a more decorative raised seam; hand sewing creates a flatter, more hidden seam.

SEWN SEAMS

A simple way to sew a seam by hand is with a whipstitch. The result is a slightly raised seam. Just place the two sweater fabric pieces wrong sides together and sew the seam with a tapestry or yarn needle, matching row to row. The more fabric picked up on either side of the seam, the more raised the seam will be.

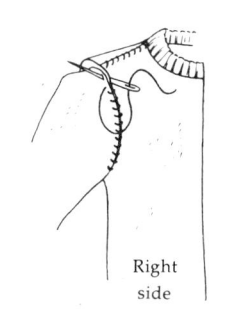

CROCHETED SEAMS

Choose a hook comparable to the hook or needle used to make the sweater fabric (see the chart, Equivalent Hook and Needle Sizes in Relation to Yarn, page 148). The yarn too should be similar or slightly lighter in weight than the sweater yarn. To accentuate seams, choose a contrasting color yarn.

Experiment with seam techniques, stitches, and colors on sample swatches to determine the combination you like best.

Crocheted seams can be worked on either the right or wrong side of the sweater craft garment. A slipstitch produces a flatter seam, whereas a single crochet makes a more raised seam. Catching both stitch loops, rather than just inserting the hook through the stitch, also gives a more decorative, raised joining stitch. (Refer to Crochet Basics, page 154.)

For knitted sweater fabric, align the two sweater pieces wrong sides together. Working in either a single crochet or slipstitch, insert the hook into both corresponding knit stitches.

Knitted sweater fabric can also be joined "stitch to row"—that is, a cast-off edge to a stitch edge.

"Stitch to row" seam

For crocheted sweater fabric, place the pieces wrong sides together. Align corresponding crochet stitch loops.

First insert the hook through the loop of each stitch on both sweater pieces. Then join with a row of slipstitch or single crochet.

MACHINE-STITCHED DECORATIVE SEAMS

THE LONG JOHN SEAM

The insides are out, but fashionably in! The long underwear look is no longer hidden under outer clothes or saved for the coldest winter days. Many ready-to-wear manufacturers are making sweaters à la long underwear. One of their underwear techniques is simply to sew sweater seams on the right side of the sweater rather than the wrong side. A trimmed zig-zag seam is best for this look (see page 53). Then zig-zag topstitching is added to necklines, cuffs, and pockets. Draw attention to Long John stitching with contrasting color thread.

Another way to fashion your sweaters in this manner is to zig-zag directly over seams. To avoid excessive bulk, straight stitch the seam first (right sides together) and press open. Zig-zag stitch on the widest setting over the seam line from the right side. Straight stitch (6–8 stitches per inch) on either side of the zig-zag with matching thread.

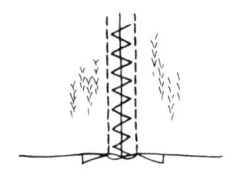

Trim the seam close to the stitching on the wrong side.

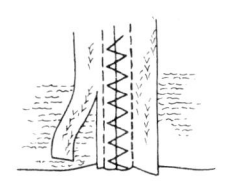

✏. LACED SWEATER SEAMS

When you're on the go, laced sweater seams travel with you. They give a distinct, handcrafted look to sweater craft garments and home furnishings. Join sweater craft patchwork with lacing too (see Patchwork Sweater Craft Projects, page 171).

If the sweater edges aren't finished and tend to ravel, work a row of whipstitches around them in matching thread. Or turn the edges under and stitch by machine or hand. If you combine sweaters with leather or fur (see page 128), "punch" the seams and then lace them.

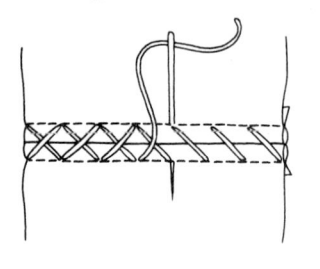

X-stitch

This is one of the most simple lacing stitches, although it looks intricate and time consuming.

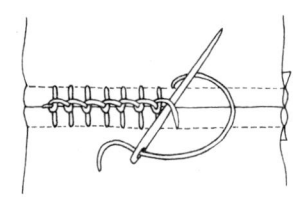

Buttonhole lacing

This is another super easy lacing stitch that gives any sweater craft garment a professional touch.

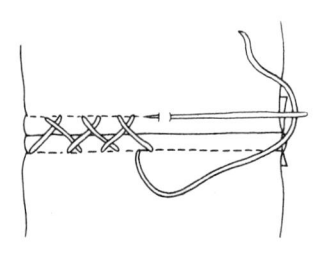

Fish-bone lacing

This is a popular seam lacing for leather, fur, and very firm sweater fabrics.

SEE-THROUGH LACE INSERT SEAMS

Want to transform a plain sweater into a sexy evening top? Or cleverly mend a tear or a hole without darning? See-through lace insert seams make any sweater, either ready-made or your own creation, unique.

Coordinate the lace weight to the sweater fabric. Heavy or stiff laces won't lie flat or conform to the contours of the figure. Remember, most woven lace doesn't stretch like sweater knits, so don't use lace seams in parts of the garment that must be pulled over much larger body curves.

Use washable laces for washable sweaters and fabrics. Prelaundering is suggested to avoid shrinkage or color-running problems.

1. Place the lace in position on the sweater fabric or garment and pin.
- Before you insert lace seam into a finished garment with an underbody or tight fit, try on the sweater to determine the lace length necessary and the placement desired. Pin the lace over body curves.
2. Baste both long edges in place with the right side up to prevent stretching of the sweater fabric, using a long zig-zag or straight stitch. 
3. Cut open the sweater fabric on the wrong side between the two basting rows.
4. Fold the raw edges back against the wrong side of the sweater. Sew again with the right side up over the first basting stitches with a narrow zig-zag or straight stitch.
5. Trim the raw edges on the wrong side, close to the stitching.

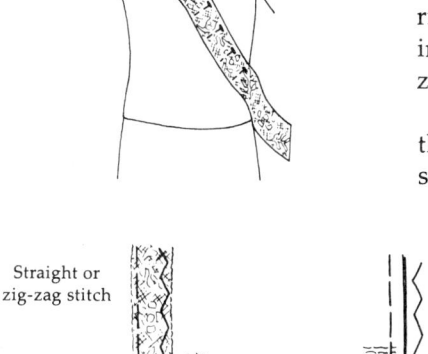

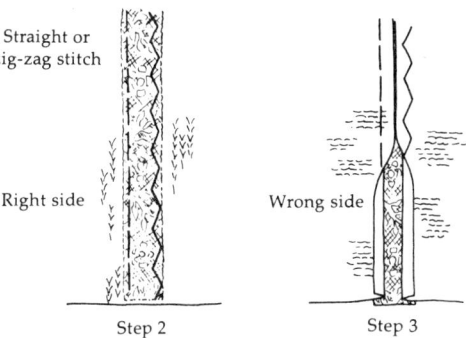

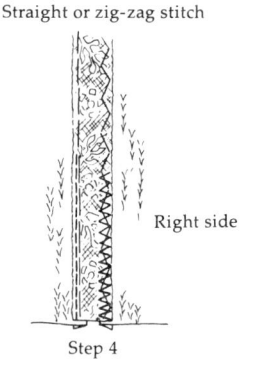

Straight or zig-zag stitch

Right side

Step 2

Wrong side

Step 3

Straight or zig-zag stitch

Right side

Step 4

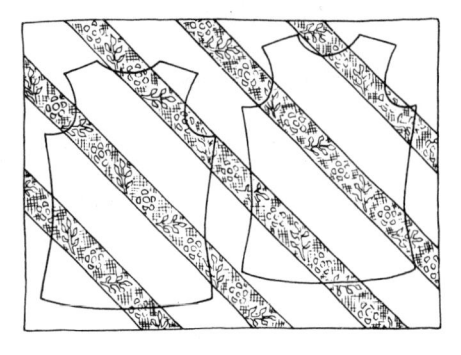

◥. LACE HEMS

To complete the see-through look, you might want to add lace to the hem.

Use the following method on heavier weight or tightly knitted sweater fabric.

1. Pin the lace ½" from the raw hem edge on the right side of the sweater fabric.
2. Stitch in place.

You can also put lace insert seams into the fabric before the garment is cut out. Place the pattern on the fabric to decide where you would like to insert the lace seams. Then seam all lace pieces following the above instructions. Lay out the pattern, then cut out the fabric. It may be necessary to match lace inserts at seam lines.

3. Trim the raw edge close to the stitching.

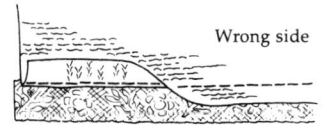

Follow these steps for lightweight or loosely knitted sweater fabric.

1. Pin the lace ½" from the raw hem edge on the right side of the sweater fabric.
2. Stitch in place.
3. Fold the raw hem edge toward the wrong side of the sweater.
4. On wrong side, stitch again over the first stitching line.
5. Trim the folded-up edge next to the stitching or topstitch in place.

Lightweight knits

NECKLINE VARIATIONS

Necklines are easily altered on most sweaters, and require little or no time-consuming facings, interfacings, or pressing. (See Chapter 3, Sweater Sewing, for basic necklines.)

Necklines are often cut slightly higher (½"–1") on the back than the front so that the neckline hugs the nape better. You can change the look of any sweater by cutting the neckline up or down before applying ribbing/trim.

Sweater Design Workshop • 95

◥. TURTLENECKS

Turtlenecks can be very tall and tight or short like mock turtles. Change the basic turtleneck by altering height and circumference measurements. Experiment with strips of sweater fabric or ribbing/trim to determine what dimensions are most flattering and comfortable for you.

The trick to turtlenecks is determining the correct allowances for double layer and fold-over styles. For example, if you want your double layer turtleneck to have a finished height of 5", allow 5" plus 5". If you want a 5" high double layer fold-over turtleneck, allow 5" plus 5" times two, or 20" altogether.

◥. COWL NECKLINES

Cowl necklines are actually droopy turtlenecks. You can lower the front neckline slightly—the amount depends on the cowl style and drape you desire. The back neckline should be cut higher than the front so the cowl hugs the nape of the neck. Make sure the neck edge seam line of both the cowl collar and bodice are the same measurement.

◥. V NECKLINES

V necklines typify the sporty sweater look: tennis, golf, hiking, or skiing. Change the V style by varying the neckline band width and depth.

Miter the V (see page 67) or lap the trim (see page 69).

Simulate a vest by sewing an insert in the V opening. The insert can be any neckline style, color, etc. Stitch in the ditch along the ribbing/trim seam to hold the insert in place (see page 57).

✎. CIRCULAR YOKE NECKLINE

Circular yokes are best for raglan sleeve styles. The sweater fabric should be stretchable enough to shape smoothly over the shoulders.

Cut the neckline and sleeves down the width of the yoke band (maximum 4″).

Next, stretch the yoke band to the sweater.

Another way to create a circular yoke is to crochet or knit it! Pick up the crochet or knit stitches after the sweater neckline has been cut down. Work in a circular pattern, decreasing stitches to shape the yoke to the neckline.

✎. KEYHOLE NECKLINE

The keyhole neckline is closed at the top with a fastener. Cut the neckline to fit the neck base, according to the style you prefer.

To make the keyhole opening, cut an oval shape along the center front fold to the neckline.

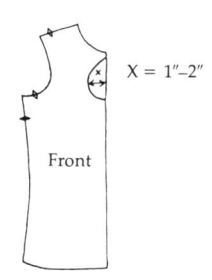

$X = 1''-2''$

Front

Finish the neckline and keyhole with binding, crocheting, or narrow ribbing. The keyhole can be fastened with a button loop (see page 102).

✎. SQUARE NECKLINE

Cut the neckline in a square shape. Square both the front and back if desired. On raglan styles the square corners should land on the sleeve seam lines. Miter the ribbing/trim at the corners (see page 56).

98 • THE SUPER SWEATER IDEA BOOK

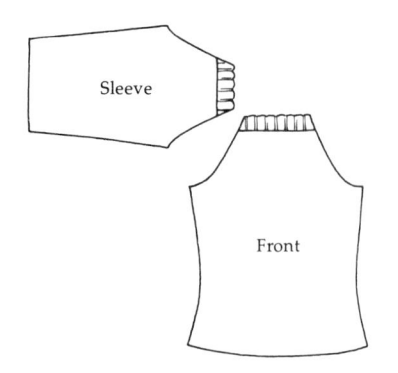

Take a square neckline shortcut: apply the neckline ribbing/trim before sewing the raglan seams so that you won't have to miter the trim to fit.

Sew the raglan seams, matching the ribbing/trim seam intersections.

SLEEVE VARIATIONS

◣. DOLMAN SLEEVE

The sleeves and bodice are cut in one piece for this style. Dolmans sew up in a jiffy. Choose stretchable and very stretchable sweater fabrics; a more stable knit won't shape to the shoulder and armscye, thus making movement difficult.

◣. RAGLAN SLEEVE

This is an easy-to-fit and easy-to-wear sleeve style. Raglan sleeves are super for oversweaters; the raglan shaping leaves plenty of room for undergarments.

For most sweater garments the raglan shoulder dart is unnecessary. The stretchability of the sweater fabric follows the shoulder contours.

SHORT-SHORT RAGLAN

An airy version that's super-cool for summer sweaters is the short-short raglan. The sleeve is joined in the raglan seams 3"–4" from the side seam. Baste and try on before shortening the sleeve. Hem the sleeve before sewing it into the armscye. Hem the rest of the underarm edge by hand or machine.

T-SWEATERS

So popular on the sweater scene today, T-sweaters are a snap to cut, sew, and fit. Usually T-sweaters are made of just two rectangular shapes joined in a T shape. The depth of the top rectangle is the same as the armscye depth (6"–11"); the width of the top rectangle determines the sleeve length.

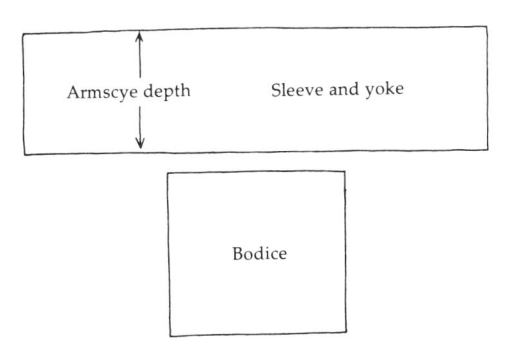

SEAMED T-SWEATER SPLIT FRONT AND BACK

Shoulder seams can be eliminated in this version. Cut two sections (each section combines the sleeve and yoke). Seam at center front and center back. Finish neck edge and hem sleeves. Join to bodice pieces.

RACING STRIPE T

Cut the top T along a wide stripe or stitch pattern. The effect is a racing stripe look that's super for active sportswear. T stripes move with you.

T-SWEATER WITH INSERT

Add a 3"–6" insert in the center front (and back if desired), shorter than the sleeve height.

Sweater Design Workshop • 101

CARDIGAN T

Start with any T pattern. Split the pattern along the center front. Lengthen the sleeves if necessary. Finish the front and neckline edges and add closing fasteners.

"SEW SIMPLE" T

This version is made in one piece without the bodice/T seam. What could be easier? Just cut out the T shape. Neckline treatments can vary—try a crewneck, a turtleneck, or a cowl. Sew the sweater together and you have an instant T!

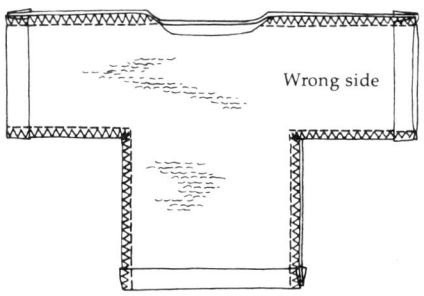

Wrong side

CLOSURE VARIATIONS

BUTTONS AND BUTTONHOLES

To eliminate the problem of stretching sweater edges, trim the edge with ribbon, leather, or woven fabric wide enough for buttons and buttonholes to be centered on. Then stitch the buttonholes by machine. These trims make it easier to produce evenly stitched buttonholes.

⌒. BUTTONS AND LOOPS

Work a row of chain stitch along one side of the opening (work on right side for women, left for men). On tightly knitted fabrics, you might have to work a row of blanket stitch along the edge before chain stitching. (Refer to Crochet Basics, page 154.)

For the button loop, chain stitch without joining to the opening edge a length just long enough to fit around the button. Then work the chain stitch back into the opening edge stitch.

Sew the buttons to the opposite opening side very close to the edge.

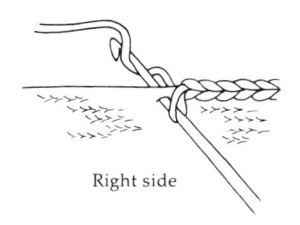

Right side

Right side

⌒. LEATHER TOGGLES

For this kind of closure, choose a style which has front pieces meeting with no overlap.

Stitch purchased toggles on with a long straight machine stitch and a leather-stitching needle. If the leather is extra-thick and hard to stitch by machine, blanket stitch the toggles on by hand with heavy duty thread or yarn.

⌒. BUCKLE UP

No, it's not seat belts! It's rectangular fastening bands made of leather or leatherlike vinyl. *Note:* Remember that leather or leatherlike trims may affect the sweater's washability. You can purchase or make your own bands. You can find buckles in most fabric stores or departments. Look for buckles that are lightweight so they won't "droop" and pull the sweater fabric.

The sweater's opening edges should meet, not overlap. The buckle band width depends upon the size of the buckle. The total band length should be between 3"–5". Allow extra length; you can trim after you try on. To make your own bands, trim ends of the rectangle in a square, round, or pointed shape. Attach the belt buckle to one end of the leather band. Sew both halves of the band to the sweater by machine using a leather-stitching needle.

✁. TIE ONE ON

You can make tie closures from finished-edge sweater trim, leather, woven ribbon, or stitched-and-turned fabric strips. Be sure to allow enough length to tie—about 4"–6" for each piece. Knot or hand stitch tie ends to finish. Topstitch onto sweater, or join in ribbing/trim seams.

BRAIDED INDIAN THONG TIES

Add ethnic appeal to any sweater with these Indian braid laces. They're perfect for sweater coats. The technique is easier than you think!

1. Cut two strips of leather (or leatherlike fabric) 20" × 2". For a two-tone effect, choose contrasting leather colors. Put the two thongs together, right sides out.

2. Shape the thongs identically by drawing the contour you like at one end and then cutting.

3. Make nine (or another multiple of three) strips in each thong for braiding (sharp scissors will cut leather).

4. Braid the two thongs. Secure the ends by circling and knotting with matching thread.

5. Place the sweater edge between the wrong sides of the two thongs. Sew all layers together by hand or by machine.

6. Make the ring through which the thong is knotted. Make one 3" braid and join ends with matching thread to form a circle.

7. Sew the ring to the sweater in the desired position (ring ends can meet or overlap).

8. To close the sweater, just knot the thong through the ring.

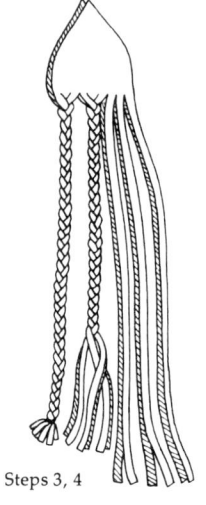

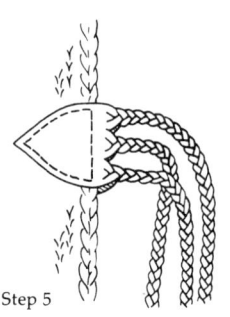

Steps 3, 4

Step 5

Step 7

COLOR PLATE 1

COLOR PLATE 2

✏. SWEATERS PLUS

Create a classic with a modern touch by combining sweater fabric with suede (page 128). The technique is easy, the results—beautiful!

COLOR PLATE 3

COLOR PLATE 4

SWEATERS FOR ALL SEASONS

In the office, on the playground, city sophisticated, or country casual . . . sweaters are for living in!

COLOR PLATE 5

COLOR PLATE 6

✎. SHOW YOUR STRIPES

Stripes are exciting, surprising, bright. Up, down, all around, stripe out in your own direction. *Color Plate 6:* Matching stripes (page 133). *Color Plate 7:* A little person's V-neck (pages 51 and 69). *Color Plate 8:* Accent with a turned-around pocket (page 134).

COLOR PLATE 7

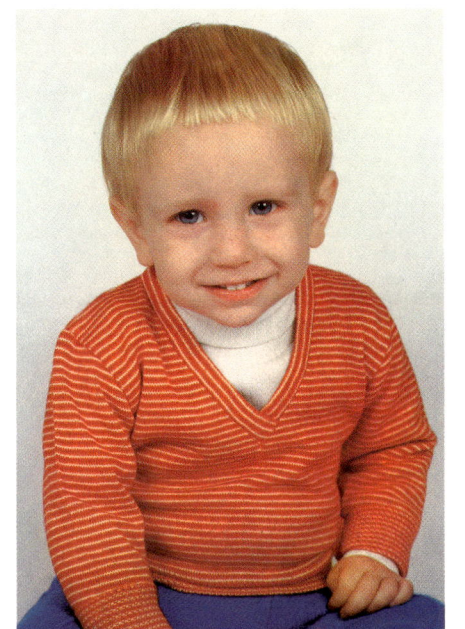

COLOR PLATE 8

COLOR PLATE 9

COLOR PLATE 10

COLOR PLATE 11

✎. SPECIAL EFFECTS

Handcrafting gives any sweater your personal touch. Embroider, appliqué, or work special edgings. Look in Chapter 4, Sweater Design Workshop, and Chapter 6, New Sweaters from Old: Recycling and Restyling, for plenty of ideas.

COLOR PLATE 12

◢. **MUCH MORE THAN SWEATERS**

Fun and fanciful sweater craft projects only take a few hours to complete. *Clockwise:* Cecil, the Funny-Faced Owl (page 195); sweater pillows (page 200); patchwork pillow (page 172); sweater craft purse (page 188); patchwork quilt (page 171); Super Sweaterman (page 197); golf club mitts (page 189).

CORD TIES

You can use cords to tie together garments, purses, or mittens. Often cords are attached to pom-poms (see page 125) so they'll hang straight decoratively! Here's how to make the simplest type—twisted cording.

1. Measure several strands of yarn, three times the desired finished-cord length.

2. Tie one end of each strand to a hook, drawer handle, or door knob. Attach the other end to a pencil or knitting needle. Pull the yarn strand taut and twist until the strand begins to kink.

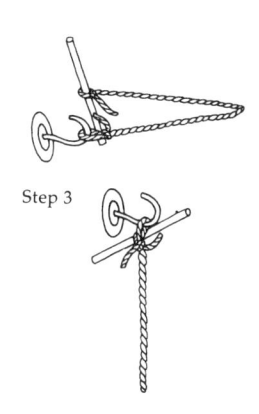

Step 3

Step 2

3. Fold the strand in half and allow it to twist.

4. Knot the end or sew to a pom-pom.

You can also make yarn cords by braiding, making macrame knots, or chain stitching. Yarn cording works well as a drawstring for necklines, sleeves, hems, and waistlines.

DRAWSTRINGS

Drawstrings are popular because they mean instant fit and fashion! Simply make a casing by turning up an edge the width of the drawstring plus ½". Thread the drawstring through and tie.

For drawstring waistlines, make a casing out of a strip of lighter weight fabric the width of the drawstring plus ½". Pin casing to the wrong side of the fabric and stitch along each long edge. Work two large buttonholes vertically in the garment to pull the drawstring through.

✎. LACE IT TOGETHER

Here's a super simple closure that works well on bulky or handmade sweater fabrics.

1. Choose a 1/8"–1/2" lacing ribbon, leather, cording, etc., that fits easily through the stitch pattern openings.
2. Draw the lacing through the stitch pattern and lace like a shoe lace or in any pattern you like. Knot the ends.

✎. IN AND OUT IN OPEN KNITS

Do you want to close a wrap style or give some extra shape to a sweater garment? If the stitch pattern of your sweater fabric is open, you can weave a decorative strip in and out of it. The strip can be made of self-fabric, trim, ribbon, leather, or any other appropriate material.

⮕. ZIPPERS

Put zippers in unexpected places such as raglan sleeve seams or the side of a turtleneck. Use a zipper as a pocket opening or as trim (apply zipper before sewing pocket to sweater).

Refer to instructions for applying various zipper types in Chapter 3, Sweater Sewing.

POCKETS

Sweaters have unlimited pocket potential. You'll find pockets an indispensable addition to any sweater and children love them too.

⮕. KANGAROO POUCH POCKET

Kangaroo pouch pockets are practical fun! You'll find many styles in commercial patterns or you can create your own. Use a sweatshirt pocket as a guideline. Apply ribbing/trim to pocket before sewing to the sweater. Place the pocket at a level comfortable for hands to rest.

⮕. ONE-STEP TRIMMED POCKET

Put ribbing or a stitch in the ditch binding (see page 57) around the entire pocket. To sew the pocket to the garment, just stitch in the ditch again. The stitching is hidden!

◣. FANCY POCKETS

Use a blanket stitch to edge the pocket and sew it to the sweater at the same time. You can complete two sewing steps in half the time! Mark the pocket placement on the sweater before stitching.

Make a large (about 5") bound buttonhole in the sweater where you want the top of the pocket to be. (The buttonhole lips are easier to handle if they're made out of leather, ribbon, or woven fabric.) Sew an inside pocket from lighter weight fabric to the lip extensions.

Experiment with unique shapes for sweater pockets—circles, squares, triangles, even animal shapes. Or for a change of pace, slant the pocket tops.

SWEATER CRAFT SMOCKING

Smocking is super simple on ribbed sweater knits. The ribbing pattern serves as a guide for the smocking intervals so there's no tedious measuring necessary!

The smocking shapes the sweater fabric to body contours—necklines, wrists, waistline, etc.

The honeycomb smocking technique draws the ribbing together in a cell-like pattern—hence the name. Each smocking stitch can be worked individually and fastened. The smocking area will be firmer, however, if two rows of smocking are completed working in one direction.

Honeycomb smocking is elastic too. You can work the smocking in thread, embroidery floss, or yarn. Yarn tends to wear the longest and has a better give with sweater knits.

Because ribbing widths vary, it is difficult to determine what size the piece will be after smocking. So smock your sweater fabric before cutting out the project. The full width of the sweater fabric can be smocked.

To keep smocking rows even, mark the smocking rows with machine or hand basting (ease plus!).

1. Draw ribbing rows together (A to B) with 2–3 even satin stitches.
2. Insert the needle into the fabric at point B and emerge at point C.
3. Join points C and D with 2–3 satin stitches.
4. Insert the needle in the fabric at point D and emerge at point E.
5. Join points E and F.
6. Continue this smocking pattern, working back and forth, row to row.

Smocking is great for children's sweater dressing—yokes, cuffs, pocket tops, and for baby caps, jackets, and sleepers.

The three-dimensional honeycomb effect makes luxurious home furnishings too—pillows in particular.

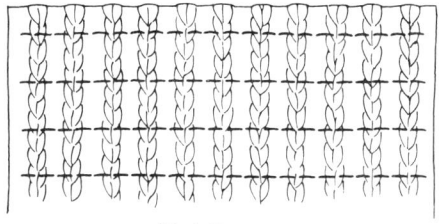

Mark the rows

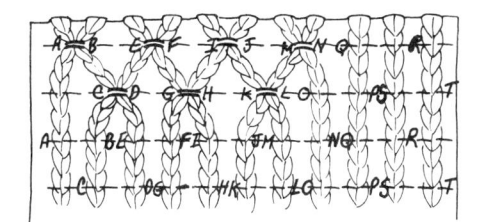

EDGING TECHNIQUES

◣. SUPER SIMPLE WHIPSTITCH

Don't think you can master embroidery edge stitches? Here's one that's beginner-proof, and can put your custom-made signature on any sweater project. You can use whipstitch edging to finish necklines, hems, pocket tops, toys, and accessories. Whipstitching can be used to sew together bulky-knit sweater seams too.

You can work the whipstitch on a raw edge that won't ravel or stretch excessively. Test whipstitching on a sample swatch edge. If you're using less stable sweater knits or you want to achieve a "rolled" look, hem before whipstitching.

Turn the edge under the seam or hem allowance width. Machine stitch (8 stitches per inch) or press in place. Do not stretch the folded edge!

To exaggerate the hem roll, insert a strand of heavy yarn in the edge fold before stitching.

To finish an edge with whipstitch, simply work from the front to the back around the edge.

BLANKET STITCH

Once used only on blanket edges, this popular stitch is currently fashionable on sweaters for the whole family. And it's quick and easy for newcomers to needlework!

This versatile embroidery stitch can make a sweater dress look more feminine or decorator pillows more rustic. The stitch variation and yarn or thread weight you choose creates an all-new edging every time.

Blanket stitching eliminates the need for hems, facings, bindings, or ribbings, and is a real fabric economizer too. Purchased sweaters and T-shirts can look handmade with blanket stitch edging.

• Select a yarn or tapestry needle large enough to thread your yarn, but small enough to be easily inserted through the sweater fabric (see the chart, Equivalent Hook and Needle Sizes in Relation to Yarn, page 148).

• On most firmly knitted sweater fabrics, preparation of the cut edge isn't necessary unless there's excessive raveling or stretching. For extra firmness, you can place a 1" strip of self-fabric along the wrong side of the raw edge. Machine stitch in place ¼" from edge. If edge stability is needed, either hand whipstitch around the border with matching thread or straight stitch by machine ½"–⅜" from the cut edge. Do not pull the edge while stitching. Use ease plus and a long machine stich, 6–8 stitches per inch, to prevent stretching (see page 52).

• On lightweight sweater knits and T-shirts turn the raw edge under ⅜" and stitch ¼" from the folded hem with the machine set at 6–8 stitches per inch. Again, do not stretch the edge while machine hemming.

• A row of machine stitching along the edge serves as a guide for stitch height.

PLAIN BLANKET STITCH

Work from left to right. Anchor first stitch at edge (A). Point needle toward you and insert in the right side of the fabric ¼" from edge. Keep thread under needle. Draw the needle downward. The distance between stitches should be consistent. See illustration for turning a square corner.

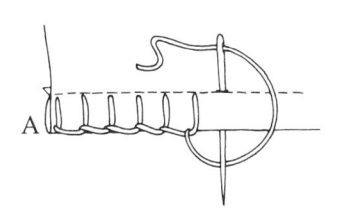

For handworked buttonholes stitch with a smaller blanket stitch very close together.

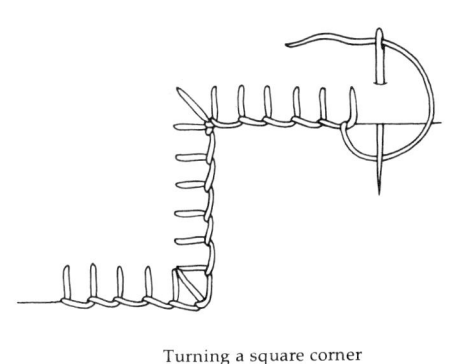

Turning a square corner

TENT BLANKET STITCH

Slant stitches to form points, resembling a row of tents.

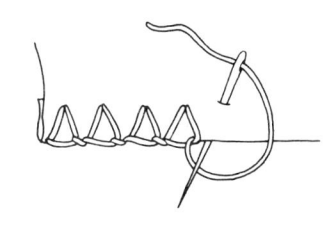

CROSSED BLANKET STITCH

Slant the stitch from right to left. Then slant the stitch from left to right over the first stitch. Place the stitches so that they cross evenly.

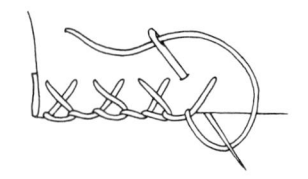

LONG AND SHORT BLANKET STITCH

Stagger the length of stitches and create your own stitch pattern. Machine stitching approximately ¼" and ½" from the edge will guide long and short stitch length.

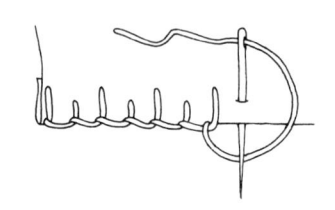

✂. CROCHETED EDGING

The handcrafted look is yours whenever you add crochet edging to sweaters. On hand-knitted or crocheted fabrics, work the crochet stitch directly in the finished fabric edge. On cut-and-sewn sweaters you have to prepare the fabric edge for the crochet edging.

The yarn used to edge should be the same or a lighter weight than the sweater fabric. The crochet hook should be smaller than the needle or hook used on the sweater craft garment itself. If the yarn or hook is larger, the edging can have a stretched-out look. (See the chart, Equivalent Hook and Needle Sizes in Relation to Yarn, page 148.)

FABRIC PREPARATION—MEDIUM TO HEAVYWEIGHT FABRICS

Cut garment where desired. Using matching thread, whipstitch along the edge to prevent raveling.

You can work a row of blanket stitch along the fabric edge first, or work crochet edging directly into the cut edge.

FABRIC PREPARATION—LIGHTWEIGHT AND JERSEY FABRICS

Cut garment where desired, allowing for a ½" hem.

Turn the hem under and machine stitch ¼" from the folded edge using ease plus (see page 52).

Work a row of blanket stitch along the hemmed edge. Blanket stitch to the hem line, placing stitches ¼" apart.

1. From the right side work one single crochet in each blanket stitch or row. (Refer to Crochet Basics, page 154.)
2. Work 2 or 3 single crochets on corners to keep the work flat.
3. To draw in the edge, skip every second, third, or fourth stitch—whatever will produce the look desired. Shape and try on as you crochet.
4. Continue until border is the width desired.

After you work the first border edging row, you can vary the crochet stitch patterns.

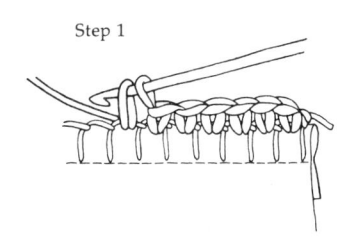

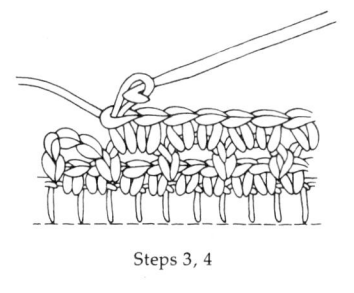

Step 1

Steps 3, 4

◣. KNITTED EDGINGS

Prepare the fabric edges as instructed for Crocheted Edging, page 120. You can pick up knit stitches through a finished fabric edge, an overcast cut edge, a crocheted edge, or a blanket stitched edge. For stability, you can single crochet around a blanket stitched edge, then pick up knit stitches.

Use a needle and yarn smaller than those used to make the sweater fabric. If you have to force the needle through the fabric, the needle is too large.

1. With the right side of the sweater fabric facing you, tie the yarn where you plan to start.

2. Working with one strand and one knitting needle, insert the point of the needle through the first stitch a short distance from the edge.

3. Wrap yarn around the needle as if to knit but draw the loop through the fabric instead.

4. Continue across edge, spacing the stitches evenly.

5. After you've picked up the knit stitches, you can knit the border. Choose a knit stitch that controls the edge and yet is decorative.

• A rib stitch (knit 2, purl 2) is a good choice for controlling fabric edges. You may need to decrease the number of knit stitches while knitting to achieve a smooth fit. (Refer to Knitting Basics, page 156.)

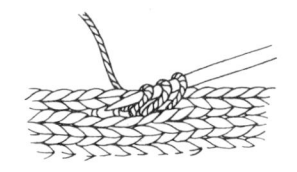

FRINGING

Fringe a shawl, a poncho, a collar, a pillow, a scarf, even a skirt! Fringing is done by hand, but it's fast.

Fringing finishes sweater fabrics without stretching the raw edge. Fringe a firmly knitted raw edge or finished hem. Or turn under the edge and machine stitch, being careful not to stretch the hem. Then fringe, using the stitching line as a depth guideline. Place fringe tassels approximately 1"–1½" apart.

SINGLE FRINGE

1. Cut yarn strands twice the desired fringe length. Usually three or four strands of yarn are used for each fringe tassel, but this varies with yarn thickness.

Sweater Design Workshop • 123

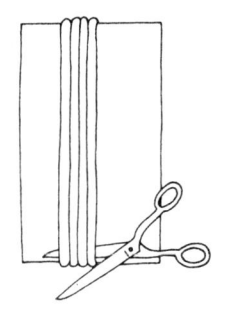

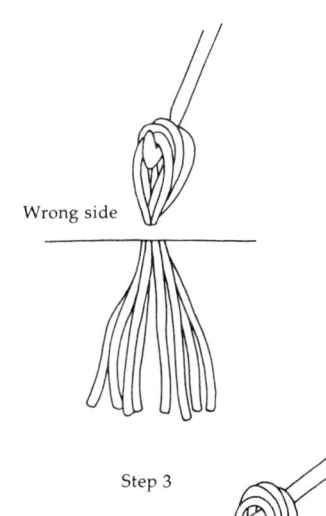

- A quick way to measure yarn lengths is to wrap the strands loosely around a piece of cardboard cut to the fringe length. Cut the yarn strands on one end.

2. Insert the crochet hook near the edge of the fabric (the hook should be small enough to fit through the sweater knit and large enough to hook the yarn strands) or thread the fringe in a yarn needle for lightweight, tightly knitted sweater fabrics.

3. Place yarn for one tassel over the hook and pull through the fabric to form a loop. Pull yarn ends through the loop and pull tight.

4. Repeat along edge at regular intervals until completed.

5. Trim any uneven yarn strands.

Wrong side

Step 3

Wrong side

Right side

SHAG RUG FRINGE

For the shag rug effect, continue to fringe in evenly spaced rows, giving sweater fabric a fur look. Add this fringe fur to sweater collars and cuffs, toys, and decorator pillows.

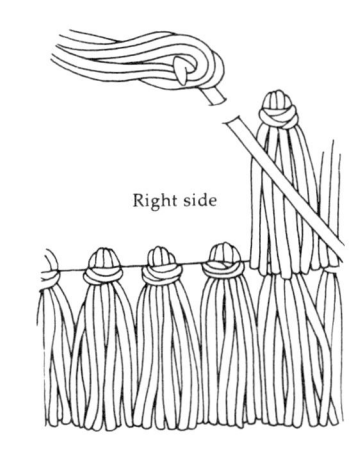

DOUBLE FRINGE

Double fringe is especially elegant on evening shawls. Customize a ready-made garment, or fringe your own creations. Sweater too short? Fringe the hem. If you're working with extra-long fringe, increase the number of yarn-strand knots.

1. Allow extra length for knotting (18" or more altogether).
2. Work single fringe along the edge.
3. Take the right half of one fringe tassel and join it to the left half of the next tassel. Wrap the first strands around the second. Pull the first strands through the circle formed. Pull down to tighten.
4. Space the rows of double fringe knots at equal intervals.
5. Trim to even strand lengths.

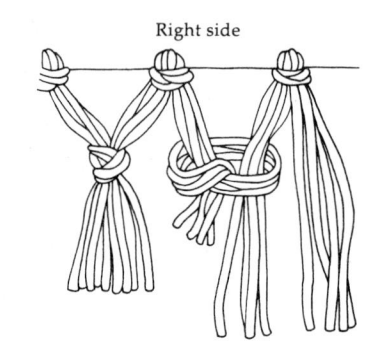

Right side

LOOPED FRINGE

This even, continuous-looped fringe can be worked along an edge, or row after row to simulate a fur or rug look.

Make the loops as long or short as you like. You can make a "ruler" out of cardboard to regulate the loop height. The ruler should be just long enough to be handled comfortably and its width should equal the desired looped fringe length. Use rulers with different widths to stagger the looped fringe length.

You can work the fringe right into the sweater fabric. Choose a crochet hook that fits into the fabric stitches without forcing. For very tightly knitted fabrics, blanket stitch the edge first, and then single crochet for added firmness. Work the looped fringe into the single crochet stitches.

Looped fringe edge stitch

1. Holding the cardboard ruler behind the edge, insert the crochet hook in the stitch or fabric.

2. Wrap the yarn lengths (approximately 3"–5") around the ruler from front to back. Draw the loop through the stitch or fabric, yarn over the hook, and draw through the remaining two loops.

3. Continue around the edge or across the row.

Looped fringe "fur"

1. Chain stitch in evenly spaced rows on the sweater fabric. The closer together the chain stitch rows are the more plush the fringe fur.

2. Work the looped fringe edge stitch into each chain stitch.

3. Continue until the entire piece is covered with fur fringe.

PUFFY POM-POMS

Top off ski hats, gift wrapping, and toys with these perfect-every-time pom-poms!

Need coordinating yarn? Blend different yarns together for a multicolored pom-pom. During the holidays, pom-poms give gift wrap a custom-crafted look.

You'll need approximately 15 yards of medium weight yarn to make one puffy pom-pom.

1. Cut two cardboard donut-shaped patterns, with diameters 1½ times the desired pom-pom size (e.g., 3" donut pattern makes 2" pom-pom). Use the bottom of a cup or bottle to draw a circle. Cut a center hole in each cardboard pattern—the larger the hole, the thicker the pom-pom (should be ⅓ of the diameter). Place the two circles

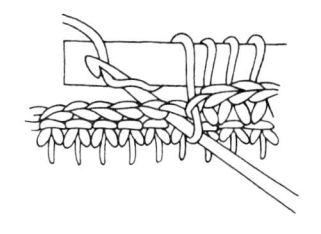

together. (You can also purchase plastic pom-pom patterns from needlecraft stores and departments, but they're available in only a limited range of sizes.)

2. Thread yarn on a large needle. Draw strands through center hole and around pom-pom pattern until the hole is filled.

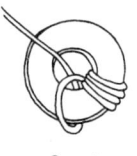

Step 2

3. Following the groove between the two cardboard patterns, cut the yarn carefully.

4. Cut one yard of yarn. Tightly wrap it twice around the strands between the patterns. Tie securely. Leave the yarn ends long for easier attachment to garments, toys, etc.

5. Fluff and trim pom-pom.

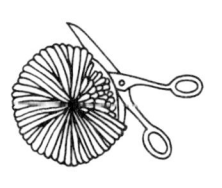

Step 3    Step 4    Step 5

More than one pom-pom at a time

Here's an easy way to mass-produce pom-poms for projects that call for several of the same thickness and color.

1. Wrap yarn back and forth between two heavy duty pins or nails on workboard. Wrap until desired thickness is obtained.

2. Tie securely at intervals slightly larger than finished pom-pom size. Leave 4"–5" yarn extensions for sewing on to the article.

3. Cut yarn halfway between each yarn tie.

4. Trim ends and fluff for fullness.

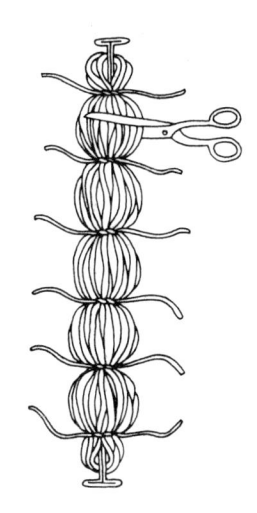

NO HASSLE TASSEL

You'll want to make these hassle-free tassels for children's caps of all kinds, toys, afghans, pillows. Tassels give edges weight and prevent them from curling up.

1. Cut a piece of cardboard 3"–4" wide and the desired tassel length. Wind yarn strands around the cardboard lengthwise until desired thickness is achieved.

2. Thread a strand of yarn through the strands along one edge and tie. Leave long threads for sewing onto article.

3. Cut through the yarn at the opposite end of the cardboard.

4. Wind a strand of yarn around all strands about ½"–1" below tied and folded end. Even up tassel end.

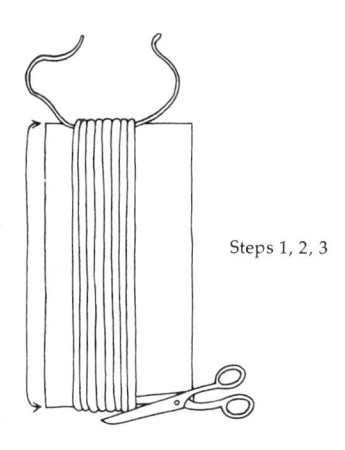

Steps 1, 2, 3

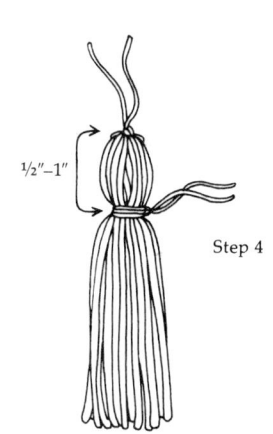

½"–1"

Step 4

SWEATERS PLUS LEATHER OR FUR

Although leathers and furs are elegant, they can be stiff and constricting, and, needless to say, expensive. The combination of sweater fabric with leather and fur adds the flexibility that makes the garment as comfortable as it is luxurious. And another advantage—you'll use less fur and leather, and save money!

Use leather trim on pockets, front bands, and cuffs. You can make a matching belt from the leather scraps!

Leather laces can close sweater edges. Just lace in and out of the fabric stitch pattern.

You can also bind and trim sweaters with leather. Leather stabilizes sweater edges. It's good for buttons and buttonholes too. Just topstitch the leather bands on with a 6–8 stitches per inch setting; a roller, walking, or even feed foot helps to move the leather under the machine stitching. Use a leather-stitching needle.

Use lightweight, flexible leather or suede, and bind the edge with stitch in the ditch binding, page 57. Or try sweater ribbing to control leather or fur neckline, hipline, and cuffs. Even hats can be trimmed with ribbing for a better fit!

✎. SWEATER FABRIC RIBBING WITH LEATHER OR FUR

When you combine sweater ribbing with leather and fur, make sure the fabric is comparable in weight and resilient enough to control the edge.

1. Fit the ribbing to the body area. A double layer ribbing works best with most leather and fur.

2. Stitch to the leather or fur, distributing the ease evenly with the ribbing side up. (The ribbing glides more easily under the machine foot.)

✎. OTHER SWEATER FABRIC SECTIONS WITH LEATHER OR FUR

You'll also like sweater fabric sleeves, collars, and cuffs in leather or fur garments. Sweater fabric adds comfort, fashion, and versatility to leather and fur.

1. Crochet or knit to fit the sweater fabric (see page 148) to pattern dimensions, or cut pieces out of sweater fabric.

2. Sew the sweater fabric to the leather or fur by machine or hand.

✎. SWEATER FABRIC SEAMS WITH LEATHER OR FUR

1. Punch holes along the leather or fur edge ¼" apart, ⅜"–½" from the edge with a leather punch or thonging chisel.

2. Work a row of blanket stitch in the punches.

3. Lace the sweater fabric (see page 91) or stitch by hand to the leather or fur. To coordinate the sweater fabric to the rest of the garment, lace all seams together with matching yarn.

4. Finish the edges with a blanket stitch and single crochet edging. (Refer to Crochet Basics, page 154.)

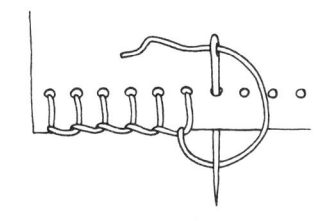

SWEATER SEAMS WITH LEATHER PATCHWORK

Leather patchwork can also be sewn or laced after being punched.

1. Work around the leather with a blanket stitch.
2. Work a row of single crochet in the blanket stitching. (Refer to Crochet Basics, page 154.)
   - To enlarge the patch size and therefore the garment size, increase the number of crochet rows worked. Crocheting can be used to form collars, cuffs, and edgings of all kinds.
3. Sew the patchwork together by hand (see page 172).

LEATHER AND FUR APPLIQUÉ

Create a scene in appliqué with leather, fur, and suede patches. Cut out the leather or fur pieces, tape them in place on the sweater, and hand stitch or zigzag around the edges.

Remember that the leather restricts the sweater's stretchability so use this appliqué method only in relatively stable garment areas such as yokes, cuffs, collars, front bands, and trims.

MIX AND MATCH SWEATER AND WOVEN FABRICS

The mix-and-match method of combining sweater fabrics with more stable wovens adds a fashionable and functional dimension to your sweater craft creations.

This method helps to coordinate a wardrobe too. Sew a woven skirt or pair of slacks and complete the outfit with a sweater trimmed in the same woven fabric. To customize any ready-made sweater, add woven yokes, bindings, and cuffs—a super way to spark up an old sweater too!

Here are some ideas to inspire mix-and-match creations. Try a combination on the bias edge, tie fasteners, plackets, bindings for collars and pockets, center or side sections on princess-style sweaters, appliquéd yokes (woven fabric is topstitched on).

⌇. LINED SWEATER JACKET

This great combination is designed for full fit sweater jackets only, since body and underbody fits would be too tight for the woven lining. Choose sweater styles with lapels and fold-up cuffs, so the lining will show!

1. Make the sweater jacket to size or purchase a sweater jacket.
2. Using the sweater pieces as patterns, cut out coordinating woven lining. Add 1" to all seam lines (⅝" for seam allowances + ⅜" for extra ease).
3. Join the lining seams.
4. Sew the sweater together. (Skip this step if you're working with a purchased garment.)
5. Place the lining inside the sweater, wrong sides together.
6. Bind the raw edge of the lining and sweater with bias trim (see Stitch in the Ditch Binding, page 57), or fold the lining seam allowance under ⅝" and blind stitch to the sweater edge.
7. You can work a blanket stitch (see page 118) in matching yarns over this edge for a fine finishing touch!

↙. QUILTED SWEATER JACKET OR COAT

Quilted sweaters are super plush and practical! Choose a striped or plaid fabric for the sweater lining so that the lining design lines can serve as stitching guidelines for the quilting.

1. Follow the cutting directions for the Lined Sweater Jacket (see page 131).

2. Using the sweater as a pattern, cut out a thin layer of fiberfill for each piece.

- Quilted sweaters are stable and bulky, so allow extra wearing ease (see page 38) in the pattern fit.

3. Place the sweater pieces on a flat cutting surface, wrong side up. Cover with the corresponding layers of fiberfill batting.

4. Place the last (third) layer—the lining fabric—right side up, on the batting and sweater fabric.

5. Quilt all three layers, stitching either by hand or machine (quicker!) along the lining design lines. Quilt as much or as little as you like.

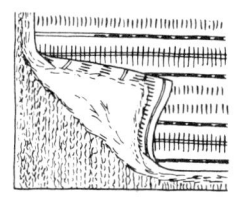

6. After quilting all pieces, sew the sweater together. (See page 52 for assembly order.)

7. Bind the edges with bias-cut lining fabric (see Stitch in the Ditch Binding, page 57).

Try unusual linings, prints, uneven stripes and plaids for quilting that's one-of-a-kind.

Sweater quilting adds texture and durability to home furnishings, like pillows and bedspreads too.

SWEATER STRIPING

Rugby stripes, racing stripes, tennis-inspired striped trims, border stripes, subtle "tweed stripes". . . . . It's hard to imagine sweaters without stripes!

Worried about matching stripes? The minimal seaming and fitting lines in sweater craft make matching easy.

Stand in front of a mirror and drape the sweater fabric on your figure. Which stripe direction is most becoming or interesting? You can create unique sweater looks by cutting stripes in different directions—up and down or around, on the bias, in chevron designs—or using unusual border motifs. Remember, you are the designer.

IT'S "SEW EASY" TO MATCH STRIPES

The secret to matching stripes is to lay out the pattern pieces on the sweater fabric accurately, matching stripes seam to seam.

After you cut out the sweater, pin the seams together, matching stripe to stripe. To prevent top seam "growth" as you sew, change to an even feed, roller, or walking foot.

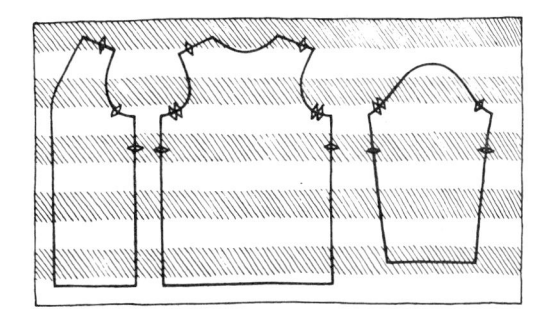

Straight stitch (8 stitches per inch), being careful not to pull or stretch seams while stitching.

Inspect the seam from the right side. If you've made a too-obvious mismatch, pull out the straight stitching and try again. Hand baste if necessary. If you straight stitch the seams first, it eliminates tedious ripping out of zig-zag or stretch stitches.

If the stripes match closely enough, the seam can be stitched again with a stretch, zig-zag, or straight stitch and trimmed (see Sweater Seams, page 53).

You can use this method for matching stripes for bias designs and chevron patchwork too.

◣. UP AND DOWN OR AROUND

Ideally, horizontal stripes that go around the figure are matched at the side seams and across to the sleeves.

With sweater fabric by the yard, just match pattern notches from front to back bodice. Then transfer stripe markings to the sleeve pattern, either along the sleeve cap or from the sleeve underarm down.

Depending on the stripe size, it might be possible to match the sleeve stripes to the sweater at both the cap and from the underarm across. Since matching is more noticeable from the front, match to the front sweater pattern first! Don't be concerned if all seams or sleeves cannot be perfectly matched. Even some very expensive ready-made sweaters are not matched at all!

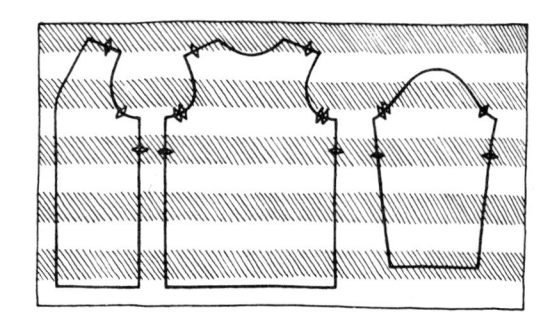

Horizontally striped sweater bodies limit matching options because of the finished hem edge. Lay out front and back pattern pieces so that side seams match. Transfer stripe markings to the sleeve pattern. Place the sleeve pattern on the sweater knit fabric and try to match either the cap or sleeve seam to the bodice stripes. The sleeve hem must be placed along the sweater body finished edge; matching might be impossible, especially if the sweater is short and the sleeve length long, or vice versa.

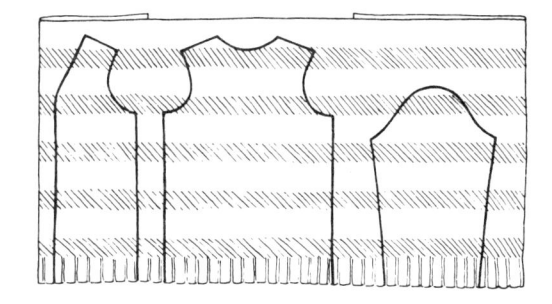

When horizontal matching is impossible, lay out main pattern pieces so that the stripes run vertically. In this way matching is unnecessary and sleeves, collars, yokes, pockets, cuffs, etc., are accented!

Another alternative to matching horizontal stripes is to cut the entire sweater with vertical stripes.

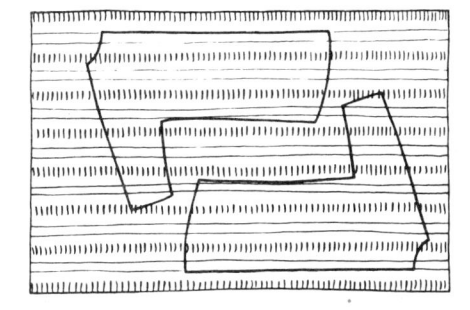

◣. SWEATERS ON THE BIAS

One of the most smashing sweaters you can sew is cut on the bias! Bias (diagonal) lines are usually more slenderizing to a larger-than-model-size figure too. So, if you have a big, bold stripe and want to avoid that "pounds heavier" illusion, cut the fabric on the bias.

To find the true bias of your pattern piece, fold the grain line in half so that it forms a right (90°) angle to itself. The new fold created is the true bias grain line. Lay out the pattern pieces following this newly formed grain line. Don't forget to "flop" pattern pieces in order to get a right and a left sleeve, front, etc.

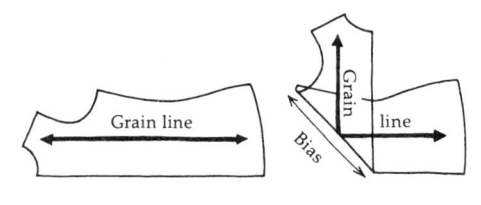

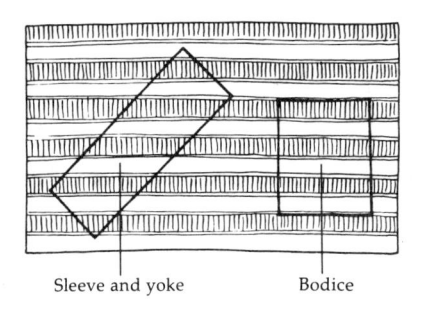

Cut sweaters or parts of sweaters on the bias: sleeves, yokes, collars. (See It's "Sew Easy" to Match Stripes, page 133.) *Caution*: Align bias stripes carefully before cutting. Mismatched bias stripes give your sweaters that undeniably homemade look!

You can use bias strips to bind sweater edges. Test for stretchability. Some bias sweater knits stretch considerably, do not recover, and therefore won't control edges. Crew necklines could "grow" into scoop necklines! (Refer to Binding for bias-binding technique, page 57.)

⚞. PLACEMENT OF BORDER MOTIF

Border striping is super for sweater separates. Drape the sweater fabric over your figure. Experiment with different motif directions—horizontal, vertical, and diagonal. Or create special effects like yoke or pocket accents with motif placement. Study ready-to-wear garments for motif-design inspiration. Unique placements of these motifs can accent, slenderize, and customize "sew" simple sweater designs. You are the designer—have fun!

Most borders call for relatively straight style lines. "A-line," fitted, flared, or gored pattern shapes can break-up the border motif. Select patterns engineered for borders. Most sweater body patterns are suitable because they've been designed for straight hemlines.

Lay out patterns on border motifs so they will match along joining seams.

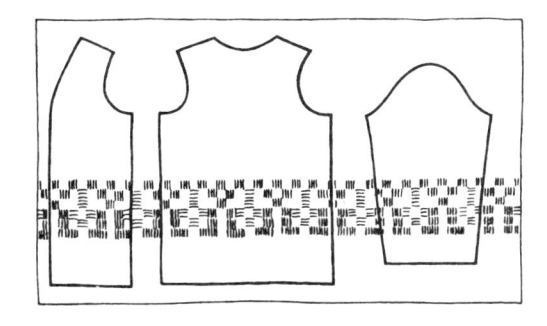

➘. "BULL'S-EYE" CHEVRON PATCHWORK

Sweater knit fabric with a definite crosswise or lengthwise stripe pattern can be cut and seamed to form a "bull's eye" chevron. You'll create one-of-a kind designs that are fashionably "on target."

Crew or boat neckline sweaters are best suited for chevron seaming. V or scoop necklines and closures would detract from the bull's-eye focus.

Add a designer accent to home furnishings with chevron patchwork on pillows, afghans, tablecloths, and bedspreads.

CUTTING ON TARGET

Fabric is seamed first, then cut out. Estimate the approximate amount of sweater fabric needed to cut out the garment pattern piece.

Divide the estimated size into equal fourths. For example, divide a 20" × 20" piece into four 10" × 10" squares. Or divide into four triangles.

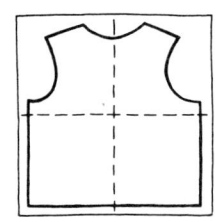

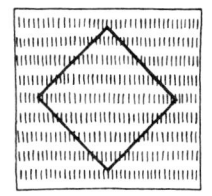

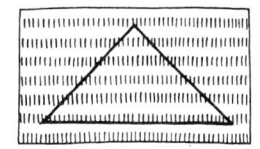

Cut out four identical bias squares or triangles. Cut triangular chevron designs so the stripes run parallel with the edge that is not seamed.

Each patch should align stripe to stripe. To make matching easier, seam two sections at a time, then join the other two, as shown in illustrations.

Focus the bull's eye chevron on the sweater front. Cut the sleeves, back, collars, etc., on the straight of the grain or from a fabric of contrasting color.

Seam two sections at a time

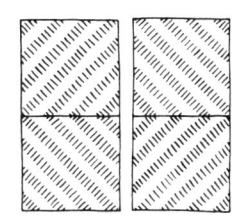

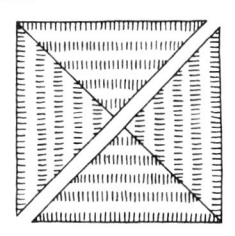

Pin the sweater pattern to the chevron design. The bull's eye is often centered on the intersection of the center front and bust/chest lines.

Before cutting, try on the chevron piece. Too much focus, especially on heavier bustlines? Adjust the chevron up or down on the pattern to find a more flattering focus point.

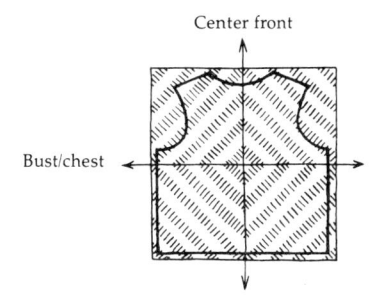

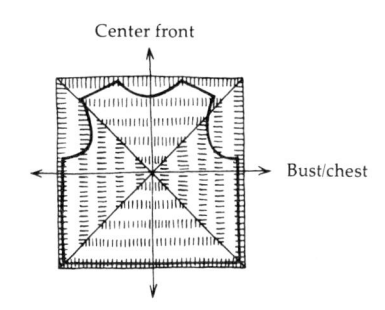

SWEATERS: THE FASHIONABLE ALTERNATIVE FOR MOTHERS-TO-BE

Tired of blousy, unattractive maternity tops? Sweater tops for mothers-to-be fit your changing shape without excess ease and fabric. Most maternity sweaters can be worn later with little or no fit adjustments.

• Select sweater fabric that's stretchable or stable; very stretchable fabric would cling too much.

• Sweater fabric by the yard is best. Avoid sweater bodies because the finished rib edge would accentuate your "fuller" areas too much.

• Choose a yoke style sweater. The fit should be full, not body or underbody (see page 18). Cut the bustline area 2"–4" larger than the pattern specifies (your measurement + 1"–2" ease + 1"–2" growth room). Flare the "baby room" to 10"–14" total ease through the torso/hipline area (your measurement + 2"–4" ease + 8"–10" "baby room"). Distribute bodice ease on the yoke piece.

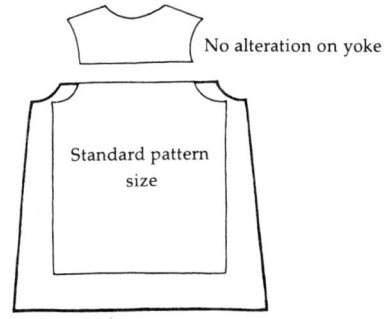

No alteration on yoke

Standard pattern size

Add 2"–3" to front length

• The sweater can fit smoothly through the shoulder and arm area. Don't make the upper body too tight, however, because it will look out of proportion to the torso area.

• Lengthen the sweater to 25"–30", which allows for the shortening caused by torso/bustline growth. Make the sweater slightly longer in the front so it will hang evenly when you wear it.

Later, the sweater can be taken in along the side seams and shortened.

CHAPTER **5**

HAND-KNITTING AND CROCHETING

There's nothing more frustrating than spending hours crocheting or knitting a sweater that, when finished, does not fit!

Rarely are sweater sizes standardized in knitting and crocheting instructions. A size 12 dress is not necessarily a size 12 sweater. And certainly, matching yarn size and stitch gauge to standard knitting or crocheting instruction is subject to human error.

The finished sweater size should never be a surprise—and won't be if you follow our crochet and knit to fit strategies. It's simply a matter of crocheting or knitting to your size rather than to instruction stitch numbers.

This chapter won't teach you to crochet or knit, but it will show you how to achieve predictable results: sweaters that fit every time with no more wasted time (or yarn!) or frazzled nerves.

TOOLS FOR KNITTING AND CROCHETING

✎. KNITTING NEEDLES

Straight single-pointed needles

These needles are made of wood, bone, aluminum, or plastic. They come in 7-, 10-, 12-, 14-, and 18-inch lengths. Sizes range from 0 (smallest) to 15 (largest). Use these needles for flat knitting when you work rows back and forth, turning at the row ends.

Circular and long flexible needles

These needles have points at each end. They are made of nylon, plastic, or aluminum. Lengths are 11, 16, 24, 29, and 36 inches. Sizes are the same as for straight needles. Use a circular needle when there are too many stitches for straight needles or use them to knit tubular articles without seams.

Double-pointed needles

These needles are made of steel, aluminum, or plastic. The aluminum and plastic ones are sized the same as single-pointed needles. The steel needles are sized in the British manner: size 15 (smallest) to size 10 (largest). Double-pointed needles are used for knitting in the round, primarily for seamless items such as socks, skirts, or mittens.

✎. CROCHET HOOKS

Standard crochet hooks

These hooks are made of bone, aluminum, or plastic. Standard length is 6". There are also wooden hooks, about 9" long (sizes 11, 13, 15).

Afghan hooks

These are extra-long crochet hooks made of bone, aluminum, or plastic. The 10"–12" length is used for crocheting the afghan stitch because the stitches remain on the hook itself.

Hand-Knitting and Crocheting • 143

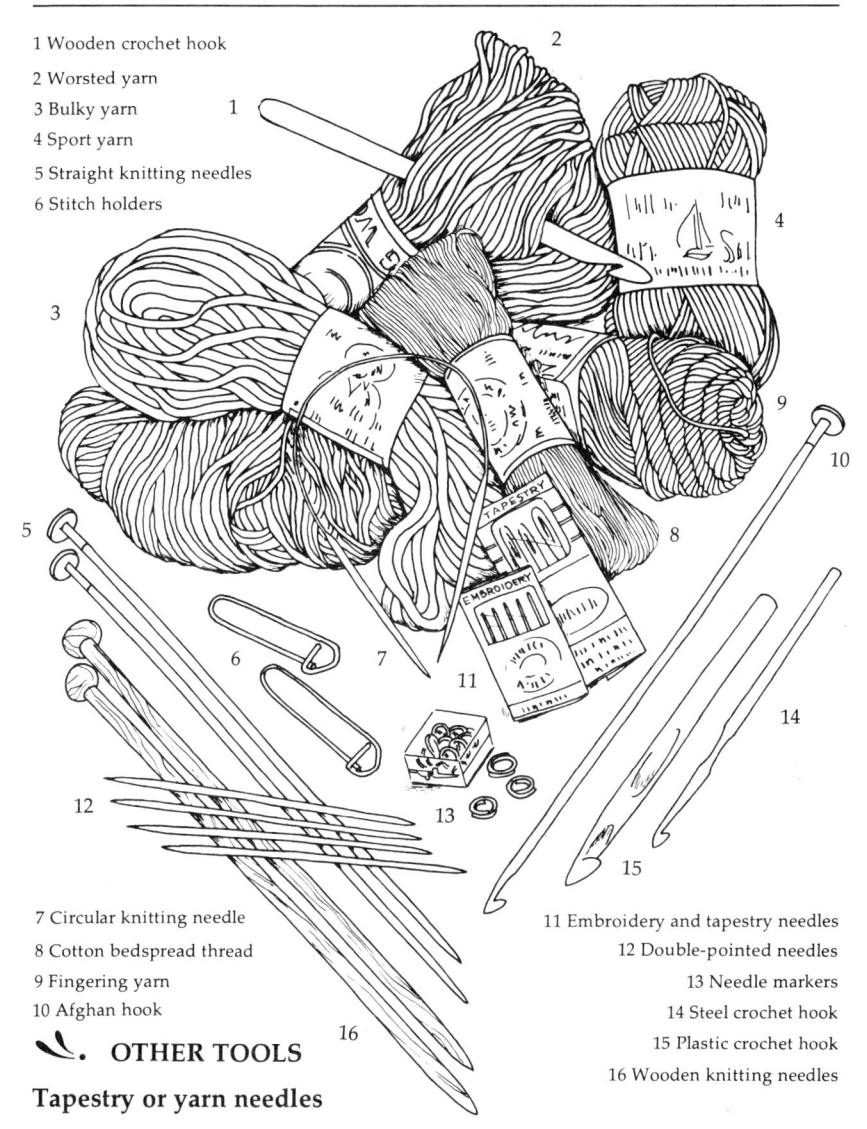

1 Wooden crochet hook
2 Worsted yarn
3 Bulky yarn
4 Sport yarn
5 Straight knitting needles
6 Stitch holders

7 Circular knitting needle
8 Cotton bedspread thread
9 Fingering yarn
10 Afghan hook

11 Embroidery and tapestry needles
12 Double-pointed needles
13 Needle markers
14 Steel crochet hook
15 Plastic crochet hook
16 Wooden knitting needles

OTHER TOOLS

Tapestry or yarn needles

These large-eyed needles have blunt points that slip between sweater knit yarns or fibers without splitting them. The needle eye should be large enough to thread the yarn easily but small enough to be inserted into the sweater fabric without creating holes. Smaller embroidery or crewel needles are used for hand stitching on lightweight, tightly knitted sweater fabric.

Stitch holders

Made of plastic or metal, stitch holders look like large safety pins. They are used for holding stitches that will be picked up later, as in neckline finishing, pockets, sleeves, and so on.

Needle markers

Used to separate sections of work, markers are helpful in some stitch patterns for increasing and decreasing, joining in different yarn colors, etc. They can be purchased or made by tying a length of contrasting color yarn around the needle. Slip markers from one needle to the other as you work.

SELECTING SWEATER YARNS

Here are some points to remember when you select yarns.

- Don't waste your time on poor-quality materials: you'll still save money making your own garments even from the best, most expensive materials.
- Buy enough yarn of one dye lot to complete the sweater craft garment. Shading can differ among dye lots of the same color.
- Yarns should not look worn or faded on the skein. Watch for pilling too. Color should be even throughout. Yarns that look worn will probably produce sweaters that wear quickly too.
- Yarn size: heavy, bulkier yarns work up faster, especially when you use large needles or hooks. However, they might feel coarse next to the skin. Lightweight, finer yarns work up more slowly but are smoother and better for close-fitting garments. Yarn weights range from very fine, for baby clothes, to bulky, for sweater coats and jackets.

Consider combining various yarn weights to achieve the desired texture and gauge.

- Yarn ply: ply is the number of strands used in yarn. Yarn that has more than one ply performs better. Two or more plies twisted together strengthens the yarn and helps to prevent pilling. The number of plies are given on the yarn label. For example: *100% Orlon® Sayelle 2-Ply Knitting Worsted.* The number of plies does not influence the yarn weight; a very fine yarn can be 2- or 3-ply.
- Yarn twist and texture: twist influences the durability of the yarn and, consequently, of the finished sweater too. Plies

twisted more tightly together secure the yarn fibers so pilling and stretching out are lessened. Too much twist results in a "hard" yarn that wears well but is abrasive to the skin.

- Yarn fiber content and care (see the chart, Sweater Fabric Fiber Content, page 25): manufacturers are required to label all yarns with fiber content and care specifications. Washable yarns are better for sweater craft garments that get soiled regularly such as children's clothes, sportswear, or tight-fitting tops. Look for colorfast yarns with minimal (1–2 percent) shrinkage. Pre-laundering is usually unnecessary for sweater yarns.
- Yarn texture: yarn texture is determined by the number of plies, degree of twist, and fiber content. Textured yarns (if not too looped or uneven) are good choices for beginning hand crafters because they camouflage uneven stitches. Avoid looped textures, however, if you're making projects that would be susceptible to snagging and pulling such as children's wear or home furnishings.
- Yarn resiliency: this is the ability to stretch and recover. Yarn that is elastic works up into projects that stretch to fit but don't sag or bag.

To test for resiliency, squeeze the skein or ball of yarn: it should come back to the original shape. Or take a measured strand of yarn and stretch it gently (some will not stretch at all) and see if it pulls back to the measured length.

You can "build in" stretchability with very stable yarns, like cottons or linen blends, by choosing very open elastic stitches, such as filet or lace crochet, rib knit, etc.

SELECTING THE STITCH PATTERN

There are hundreds of stitch patterns for both crocheting and knitting. Look in your local needlework shop for "stitch dictionaries" that give the how-tos for the various stitches.

The stitch pattern influences the following:

- Style of the garment (see page 50).
- Texture and stretchability of the fabric. After making a sample test swatch of the stitch, test for stretchability to determine which stretch category the fabric falls into (see page 19).
- Degree of difficulty in working the stitch, decreasing, or increasing.

For your initial crochet or knit projects, choose fairly simple crochet or knit stitch patterns.

The more complicated the stitch, the more difficult the decreasing and increasing calculations, and the more time the sweater takes to finish.

CROCHETING OR KNITTING STITCH GAUGE

Chances are if you have never established a stitch gauge when crocheting or knitting, you've made a lot of sweaters that don't fit. Stitch gauge is the one factor too often overlooked but vitally important to proper fit.

Because crocheting and knitting are very personal crafts, stitch gauge results vary tremendously from one individual to another. In fact, even daily, a person's stitch gauge might change with moods; for example, anxiety can cause a person to work the stitch more tightly.

Make an 8" × 8" test swatch in your chosen stitch pattern and yarn. This swatch size is larger than usually recommended. It will, however, allow you to work into a "natural rhythm" with the hook or needle size and yarn. Your stitch gauge in this larger swatch will closely resemble the actual gauge produced in making the garment.

To arrive at the gauge, measure *at the center of the swatch* horizontally, to determine how many stitches there are in a one-inch or two-inch space, and vertically, to determine how many rows measure one or two inches.

This stitch gauge becomes the basis for size and shaping calculations: sweater length and circumference measurements are determined by the stitch gauge.

Do not try to adjust your crocheting or knitting tension to meet a specified gauge because you'll eventually return to your own gauge, and the final measurements will come out wrong. Adjust, instead, the hook/needle or yarn size.

If you are attempting to match a predetermined gauge specification given in an instruction book, change the hook or needle

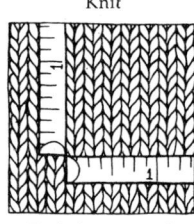

Knit

5 stitches per inch
7 rows per inch

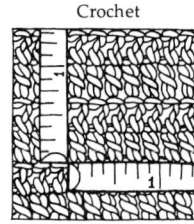

Crochet

5 stitches per inch
3 rows per inch

size until the exact stitch gauge is achieved. Too few stitches per inch means that you need a smaller hook or needle. Too many stitches per inch means you need a larger hook or needle.

If you still cannot match the gauge, try changing the yarn size.

Usually when you match the gauge stitch-wise (horizontally), you'll also match row-wise (vertically). It is more important to match the width (number of stitches per inch) than the length (number of rows per inch). You can adjust the length as you crochet or knit much more easily than the circumference or width.

• The same yarn, in different colors, can produce different stitch gauges. Sometimes the dyeing process makes the yarn heavier, sometimes thinner, or more compacted. Make a test swatch of each color, if they're used in significant amounts in the sweater.

• When *knitting* a sample swatch, do not bind off because this tends to draw in the knit swatch and distort the stitch gauge measurement.

EQUIVALENT HOOK AND NEEDLE SIZES IN RELATION TO YARN

Use the following chart when adjusting your stitch gauge larger or smaller. Remember the size of the hook or needles you use really does not matter as long as the gauge is correct. If your work is too loose, use a smaller hook or needles to tighten the gauge. If your work is too tight, use a larger hook or needles to loosen the gauge.

The chart will assist you in coordinating the hook or needle size to your yarn, but it is only a guide and you should choose hook and needle size according to the finished look desired, your stitch pattern, and your gauge.

The chart can also be helpful for choosing hook or needle size for edge finishes. The hook or needles should be an equivalent or slightly smaller size than that used on the sweater garment unless you want a ruffled or flared-edge finish. Yarn for edgings should also correspond to the fabric or be a slightly lighter weight.

Note: Crocheted or knitted edge finishes should prevent hems, necklines, closures, etc., from stretching out during wear and care. Adjust hook or needle and yarn size for proper edge control.

EQUIVALENT HOOK AND NEEDLE SIZES IN RELATION TO YARN

Crochet Hooks American	British	Knitting Needles American	British	Yarn Type
	1.75	1	2.50	Dress yarns, ribbons
	2.00	2	2.75	Baby or fingering yarns
			3.00	
	2.25	3	3.25	Baby or fingering yarns
B/1	2.50	4	3.50	Lightweight sport yarns
B/1	2.75	5	4.00	Sport yarns
C/2	3.00	6	4.50	Sport yarns
D/3	3.25	6	4.50	Sport yarns
E/4	3.50	7	5.00	Yarns slightly lighter than knitting worsted but heavier than sport yarns
F/5	4.00	8	5.50	Knitting worsted weight yarns
G/6	4.50	9	6.00	Yarn combinations ⎫ Progressively
H/8	5.00	10	6.50	Yarn combinations ⎬ heavier
H/8	5.50	10½	7.00	Yarn combinations ⎭ in weight
I/9	6.00	11	7.50	Heavyweight yarns
J/10	6.50	12	8.00	Heavyweight yarns
K/10¼	7.00	13	8.50	Heavyweight yarns
N/13	7.50	15	9.00	Bulky yarns

Although the hooks and needles listed in the chart are the most frequently called for in sweater craft, there are even larger tools and broomstick lace pins available. American crochet hooks go all the way up to 16 and Q. You can find American knitting needles sized 17, 18, 19, 35 (¾"), and super jumbo 50 (1"). The large hooks and oversized needles are great for sweater coats, afghans, wall hangings, or any project requiring multistrand yarns.

CROCHET OR KNIT TO FIT

If you're crocheting or knitting to fit your own pattern, there is no specified gauge to match. You only need to establish it. Your personal taste and the sweater's end use determine the stitch size and tension.

Try different hook or needle sizes and yarns until you produce the desired look. Again, after determining the hook or needle size and yarn type, make an 8" × 8" test swatch. Measure the gauge, both stitch-wise and row-wise. Make note of the gauge.

For your first crochet or knit to fit project, choose a basic stitch pattern with a medium to large gauge, so calculations will be elementary and the crocheting or knitting fast.

If you're working with "mystery" yarns that are not labeled for fiber content, test launder and steam press the 8" × 8" sample. Does the sample come back to size after being laundered and pressed? Or does the swatch shrink or stretch out of shape? Make size adjustments accordingly. You might decide not to use the yarn at all after testing!

CHOOSING THE SWEATER PATTERN AND SIZE

When crocheting or knitting to fit, there are many more sources for sweater patterns than needlecrafters realize.

STANDARD KNITTING OR CROCHETING INSTRUCTION BOOKS AND MAGAZINES

These publications are a popular and good source for sweater style inspiration, but be cautious of sizing. The sweater designers have their own ideas on how sizes should fit, including the amount of sweater ease. Also, allowances are not made for yarn substitutions.

Always match the specified stitch gauge. See the chart Equivalent Hook and Needle Sizes in Relation to Yarn, page 148. Convert the standard instructions into a life-size basic pattern (which is particularly helpful when you are crocheting). It's not as hard as you think!

Graphing sweater patterns

Just convert the stitch gauge for your size to flat-pattern dimensions on butcher paper or nonwoven interfacing. Pre-ruled nonwoven interfacing is available and cuts down on your graphing time.

For example, if the stitch gauge is 4 stitches per inch, 3 rows per inch, the graph for a pullover style is as follows.

Graph the sweater sleeves, pockets, yokes, etc., in the same manner.

150 • THE SUPER SWEATER IDEA BOOK

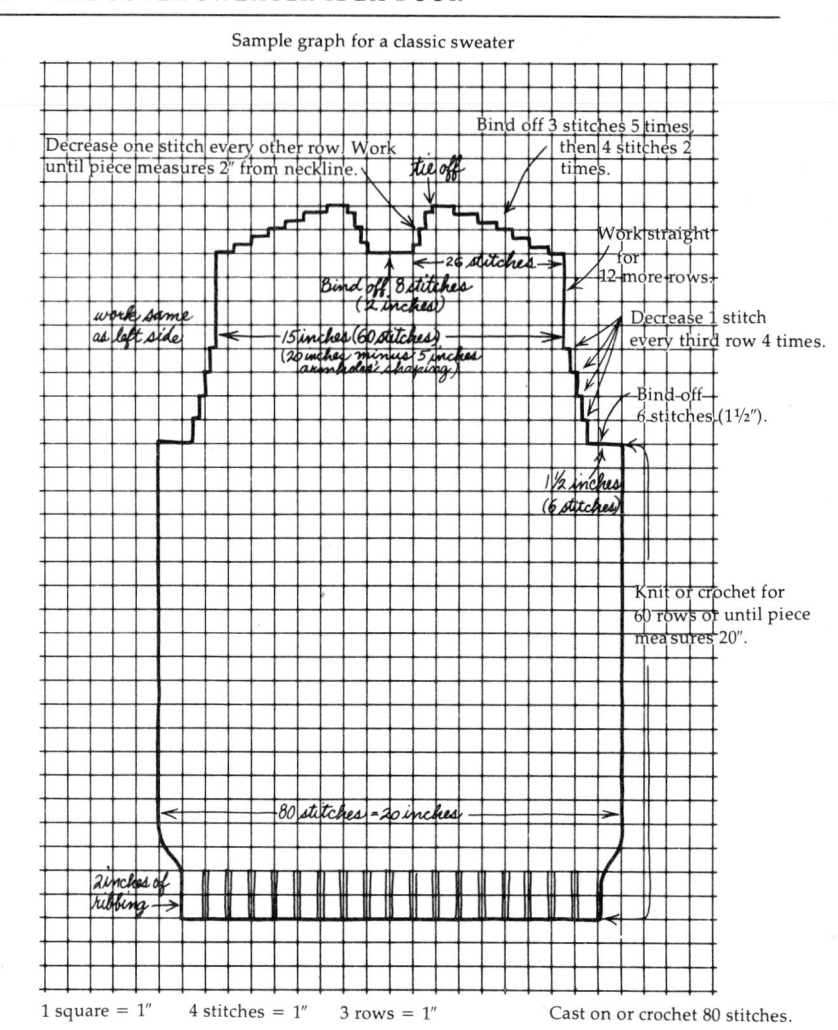

Sample graph for a classic sweater

Decrease one stitch every other row. Work until piece measures 2" from neckline. *tie off*

Bind off 3 stitches 5 times, then 4 stitches 2 times.

←26 stitches→

Bind off 8 stitches (2 inches)

work same as left side

←15 inches (60 stitches)→
(20 inches minus 5 inches armholes shaping)

Work straight for 12 more rows

Decrease 1 stitch every third row 4 times.

Bind off 6 stitches (1½").

1½ inches (6 stitches)

Knit or crochet for 60 rows or until piece measures 20".

←80 stitches = 20 inches→

2 inches of ribbing →

1 square = 1"   4 stitches = 1"   3 rows = 1"   Cast on or crochet 80 stitches.

After you have graphed the sweater pattern to scale, measure it. Compare the measurements to your own body dimensions plus wearing ease (see page 38). The stretchability of the sweater fabric or stitch determines the amount of wearing ease needed in the sweater pattern. Stretch the 8" × 8" test swatch in the crosswise direction (around the body) to categorize the stretchability: stable, moderately stretchable, or very stretchable.

Then make any size adjustments on the graphed pattern (see page 38). Translate these alterations to the crocheting or knitting instructions. For example, if the stitch gauge is 4 stitches per inch, 3 rows per inch, and the comparison of measurements shows 2" more are needed for the hipline, add 4 stitches to the back and 4 stitches to the front sweater bodice hipline (1" each piece).

This takes a little time but certainly is worth the hour or so invested when the sweater fit is ensured! After you have graphed the instructions for size, save the pattern because it can be used again as a crochet or knit to fit pattern.

Here's an example of how being off-gauge can make a significant difference in the sweater size. If you are off $\frac{1}{4}$" (plus or minus) every 2", a size 40 sweater could measure 5" larger or smaller than desired (40" ÷ 2" = 20. 20 x $\frac{1}{4}$" = 5" stitch discrepancy.)

EUROPEAN CROCHETING AND KNITTING INSTRUCTIONS

Needlecrafters who have discovered the goof-proof crochet and knit to fit method can also discover the advantages of using European crocheting and knitting patterns and instructions.

These instruction books and magazines have done the sweater pattern graphing for you! Although stitch gauges are specified, the graphed pattern makes it super easy to crochet and knit to fit.

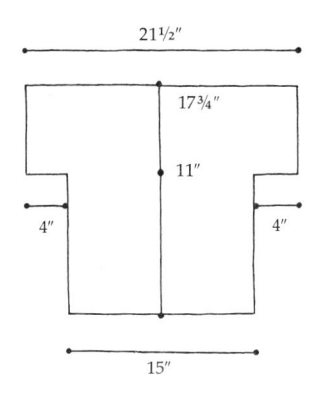

Enlarge the pattern to life size so that it can be the fitting blueprint for crocheting or knitting. A size 10 is usually graphed.

Compare your measurements to those of the graph, allowing for wearing ease (see page 38). Alter the size and number of stitches accordingly, as previously instructed for standard crocheting or knitting patterns (see page 150). Don't forget to take into account the fabric's stretchability! Once the size has been adjusted and the pattern perfected, this graph can be used for knitting, crocheting, or even sewing (add seam allowances) sweaters of similar stretchability.

COMMERCIAL SEWING PATTERNS

Here's a real breakthrough for people who like to crochet and/or knit but can't find the styles they like in standard needlework instruction books.

Choose a basic commercial pattern for all, or part, of your sweater. Look for straight lines, minimal seaming, and patterns designed for stretchable fabrics (see page 18). The selected pattern, after being altered to fit, is the fitting blueprint.

Next, establish your stitch gauge, for both stitches and rows. After measuring the flat pattern and computing the stitches necessary to shape the design, write your own knit or crochet instructions. Since the human figure is basically symmetrical, whatever stitch variation is done on one side should also be repeated on the other.

Transfer the commercial tissue pattern to butcher paper or iron to fusible nonwoven interfacing to prevent tearing.

For contour-fit ribbing on hipline, waistline, wrists, armholes, etc., use smaller size hooks or needles to tighten the stitch gauge.

Make minor adjustments as you crochet or knit to fit the pattern. Make note of the adjustments on the pattern so you'll make the same changes on the corresponding side or piece.

Caution: If you are crocheting or knitting a stitch that has a definite right or wrong side, be sure to "flop" the instructions to produce a right and a left side of each section.

Hand-Knitting and Crocheting • 153

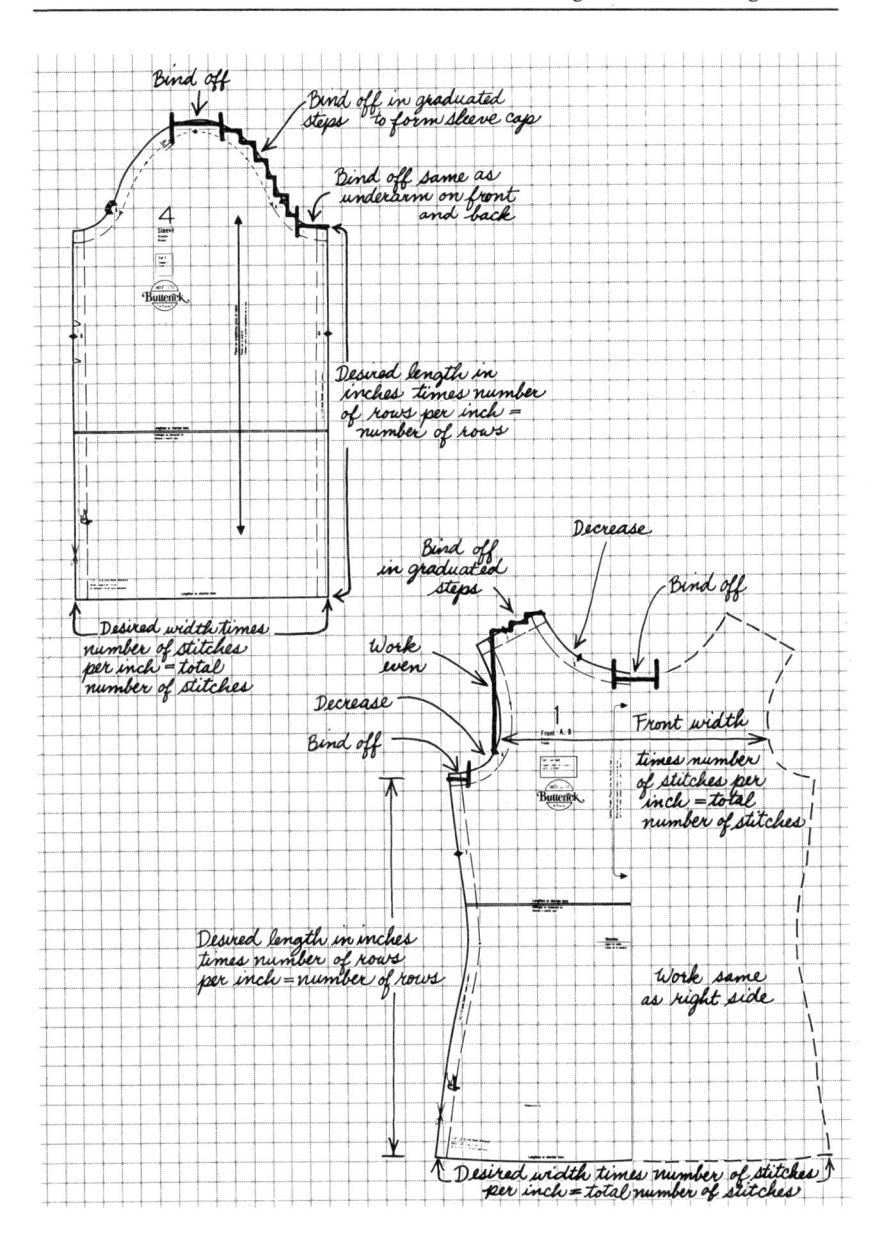

1 square = 1"

CROCHET BASICS

◞. SLIP KNOT

The slip knot begins a chain. Using the illustrations as a guide, form a circle of yarn and cross it with the yarn attached to the skein. Pull the center yarn through the circle and tighten it on the hook.

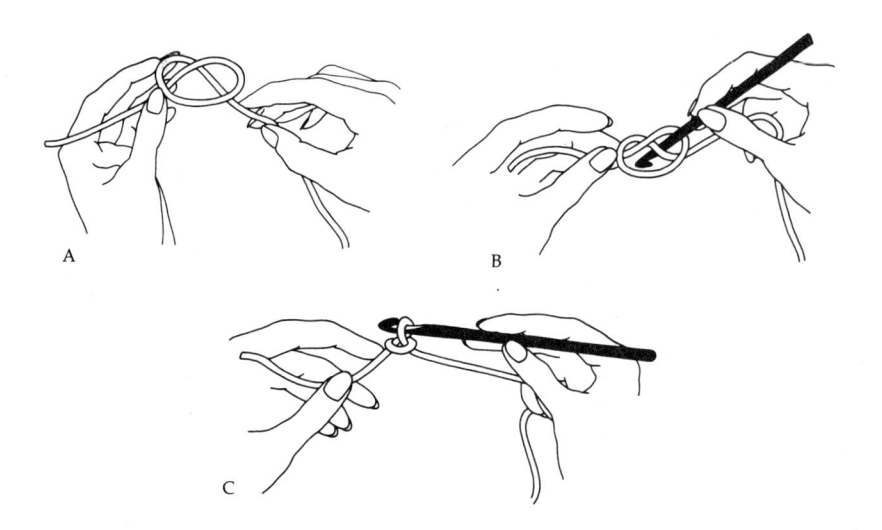

◞. CHAIN STITCH

Place the main length of yarn over the hook, then draw the yarn and hook through the loop (first stitch). Repeat for the desired number of stitches.

◞. SLIP STITCH

To advance the stitch while skipping a space, insert the hook in the stitch, yarn over and draw through the stitch and through the loop on the hook.

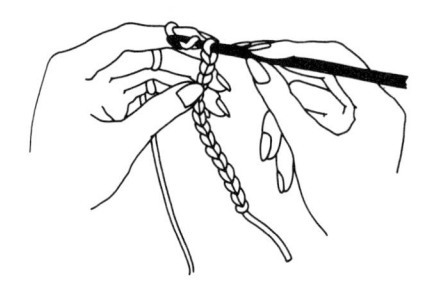

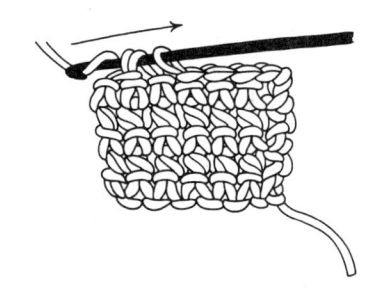

➷. SINGLE CROCHET

Insert the hook in the second chain from the hook, yarn over, and pull a loop through the chain. Yarn over again and pull another loop through the two loops on the hook.

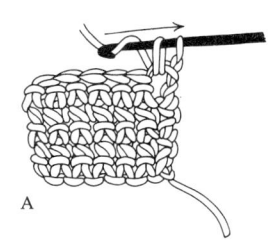

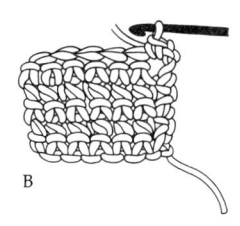

➷. DOUBLE CROCHET

Yarn over the hook, insert the hook in the fourth chain from the hook, yarn over and pull a loop through the chain. Yarn over and pull the yarn through the two loops on the hook. Yarn over and pull the yarn through the last two loops on the hook.

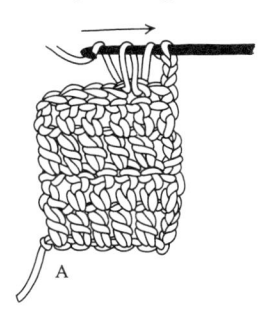

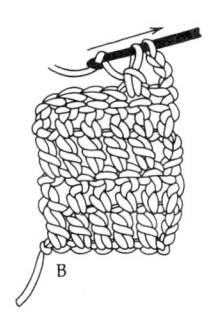

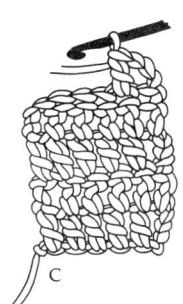

➷. TREBLE CROCHET

Yarn over the hook twice, insert the hook in the fifth chain from the hook, yarn over and pull a loop through the chain. Yarn over and pull yarn through the two loops on the hook. Repeat two more times.

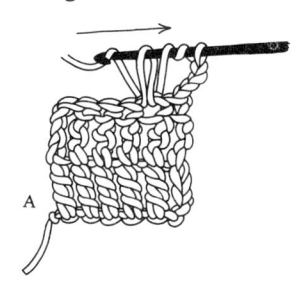

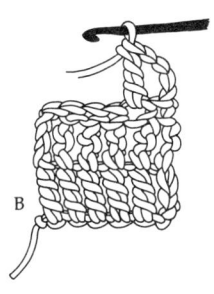

KNITTING BASICS

⌇. SLIP KNOT

Leave enough yarn to cast on the desired number of stitches. Make a slip knot on the needle.

Pull the yarn to the end to tighten.

⌇. CASTING ON

Hold the needle with the knot in your right hand. Slip your left index finger and thumb between the two strands and spread them out. Bring your left thumb up to form a loop on your thumb.

Insert the needle through the loop on your thumb from front to back.

Take the yarn from the skein over the point of the needle and draw it through the loop.

Remove your thumb from the loop and tighten the stitch on the needle. Repeat until the required number of stitches are on the needle. Do not cast on too tightly.

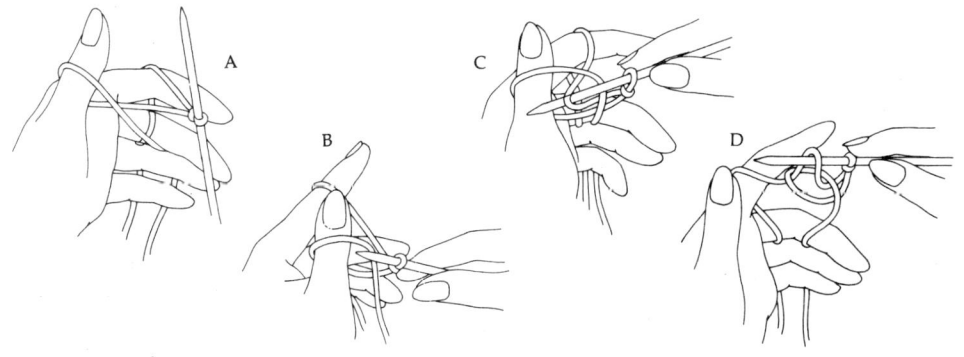

⌇. KNIT

Hold the needle with the stitches in your left hand. Hold the second needle in your right hand and thread the yarn from the skein through the fingers of the right hand.

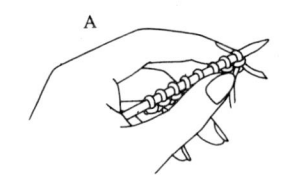

Insert the second needle into the first stitch on the left needle, from front to back.

Wrap the yarn from the skein under then over the right needle.

Draw the yarn through the stitch.

Slip the stitch off the left needle. Repeat as needed.

➣. PURL

Hold the needle with the stitches in your left hand. Hold the second needle in your right hand and thread the yarn from the skein through the fingers of the right hand. Insert the needle into the first stitch on the left needle from back to front. The right needle is in front of the left needle and the yarn is in front of the work.

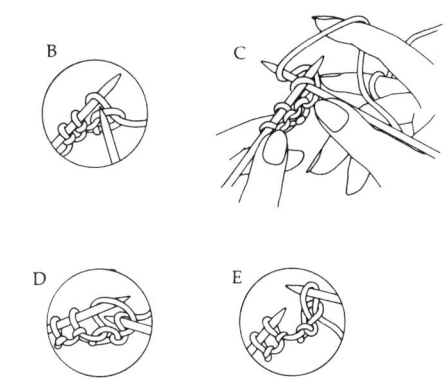

Wrap the yarn from the skein under then over the right needle.

Draw the yarn through to the back of the stitch.

Slip the stitch off the needle.

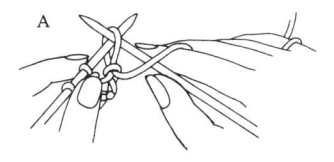

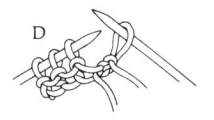

➣. BINDING OFF

Work two pattern stitches. With the left needle lift the first stitch worked over the second stitch, then off the needle. Repeat as necessary. Cut the yarn at the end about three inches from the last stitch and pull through the last loop to tie off.

• If binding off at the beginning or middle of a row, do not break the yarn off. Continue working in the pattern beyond the bound off stitches.

⚞. INCREASING AND DECREASING TO SIZE

Once the pattern blueprint and instructions have been altered for proper fit, the crocheting and knitting should be quicker!

The following techniques are basics for increasing and decreasing when you crochet or knit to fit. The techniques are numerous and vary with the stitch type. Borrow increasing and decreasing techniques for more complicated stitches from instruction books, then develop your own crochet or knit to fit designs.

CROCHETING: INCREASING

In the middle of a row: Simply work two stitches in the previous stitch. When the pattern stitch is fancy, work two patterns in one stitch.

At the beginning or end of a row: Work across the row to the end. Omit the turning chain.

Chain the number of stitches needed to increase, plus the turning chain (the number of chains needed to turn increases with the stitch size).

Work in stitch pattern across the chain stitches to the end of the row.

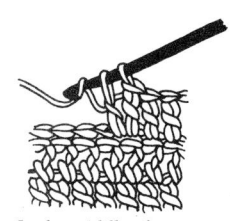

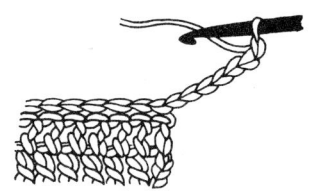

In the middle of a row

At the beginning or end of a row

CROCHETING: DECREASING

For single crochet: Pull a loop through the next stitch and the one after. Then yarn over and pull loop through the three loops on the hook.

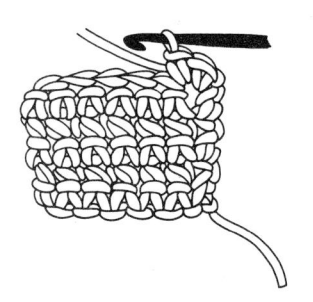

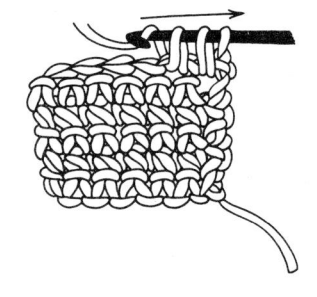

Alternate crochet decreasing method

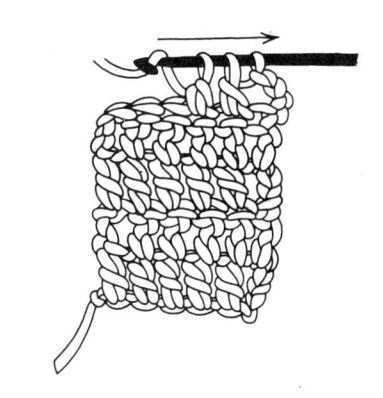

When you work with large crochet stitches (double or triple treble) this method prevents the skipped stitch gap that can result from the first method. In this alternate method, at the end of the row, work the turning chain (that acts as the first stitch of the next row).

Work in the next crochet stitch, but omit the last step. Two loops should remain on the hook.

Then, work the next stitch, also omitting the last step. There should be four loops on the hook.

Yarn over the hook. Draw the yarn over loop through all four loops on the hook. One loop should remain on the hook. You have decreased the two stitches into one, at the top of the stitch, avoiding the skipped-stitch gap at the stitch base.

Repeat the method at the end of the row: work together the second and third stitches from the end of the row. The last stitch can be worked in the usual way.

Crocheting: decreasing several stitches

At the beginning of a row: To decrease several stitches slip-stitch over the specified number of stitches to be decreased. Work one or two chain stitches before proceeding with row.

At the end of a row: To decrease, just work to within the number of stitches to be decreased. Turn and work back across in the usual way.

KNITTING: INCREASING

In the middle of a row: Knit one stitch as usual but retain the other stitch on the left needle.

Then knit a second stitch into the back of the same stitch. Slip off old stitch.

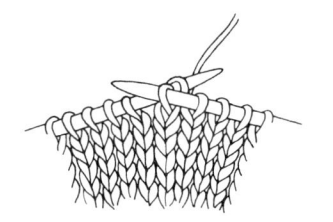

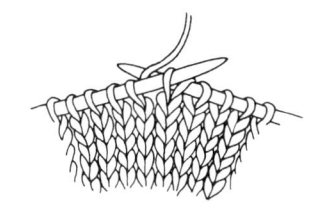

At the beginning or end of a row: Loop yarn around point of needle, as shown in illustration.

KNITTING: DECREASING

There are two ways to decrease. These instructions are given for right-handed knitters.

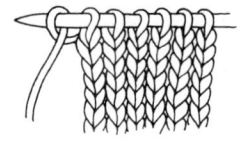

Method 1: Knit two stitches together.
Or purl two stitches together.

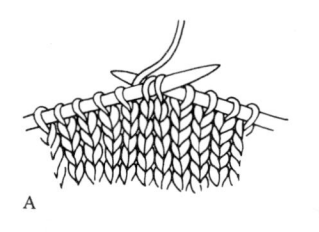

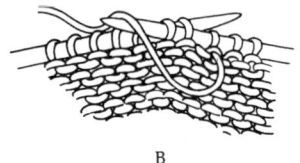

A

Method 1

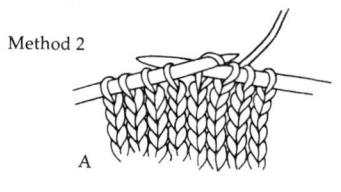

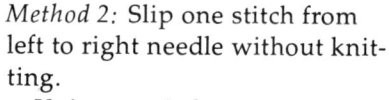

B

Method 2

A

B

Method 2: Slip one stitch from left to right needle without knitting.
Knit one stitch.
With help of left needle, pass the slipped stitch over the knitted stitch.

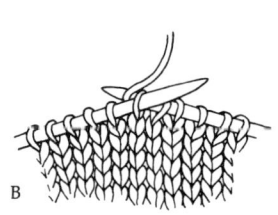

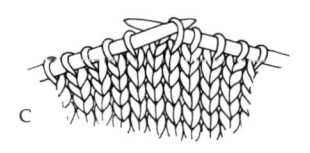

C

As you decrease and increase to fit the pattern, continually compare the shape to the blueprint size. Stretching or pulling is cheating!

It's better for the fabric to be *slightly* larger than too small; the sweater can always be taken in when assembled. If the measurements seem to be way off, double check the stitch gauge.

Take the blueprint with you when you travel too. You'll crochet and knit to fit on the go!

After the sweater is finished, use the blueprint for blocking.

BLOCKING SWEATER CRAFTS

Blocking your sweater craft garments, especially those that are hand-knitted or crocheted, can even out surface textures (and stitch imperfections) and control the project size. Block pieces to size before assembling them.

Shape the fabric to fit the sweater pattern or measurements. Blocking is easiest when the sweater pattern or desired finished shape is traced on to butcher paper. Pin the sweater fabric pieces to fit these outlined dimensions.

To prevent sweater fabric shine, pin the pieces right side down on a padded surface.

Most sweater knits, either handmade or purchased, should be steamed (with an up-and-down motion) rather than pressed. Steaming and a damp cloth prevent scorching and flattening of raised pattern stitches. Do not remove the pins until the sweater fabric is cooled and the shape is stable.

Follow this fiber content blocking chart for all sweater craft projects (see the chart, Sweater Fabric Fiber Content, page 25).

BLOCKING

Fiber Content	Press Cloth	Iron Temperature Setting
Acrylic (minimal blocking is possible, but acrylic sweater fabric bounces back to the original shape when washed)	Damp cloth	Lowest steam setting (caution: acrylic shines and scorches easily).
Angora	Very damp cloth	Low steam setting (wool). Do not use any pressure; just hold iron over sweater fabric.
Cotton	Damp cloth	High steam setting (cotton).
Mohair	Very damp cloth	Low steam setting (wool). Press lightly.
Nylon	Dry–slightly damp cloth	Low steam setting (nylon)
Wool	Damp cloth	Low steam setting (wool).
Wool blends (with synthetic fibers)	Damp cloth	Low steam setting (wool). Press lightly.

Note: Sweaters can also be professionally blocked by dry cleaners, although good results are seldom guaranteed. Be very specific when designating length and width measurements. You can even provide your dry cleaner with the crochet or knit to fit pattern for true-size blocking.

ASSEMBLING SWEATER CRAFT GARMENTS

Baste the sweater pieces, wrong sides together, along all seam lines. Try on the sweater and mark any minor fitting adjustments with basting thread (don't use pins since they tend to get lost). See page 50 and following for assembly order.

Taper any stairstep seams for an even seam line.

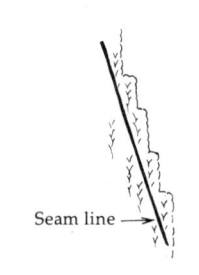

Seam line

ASSEMBLING BY HAND

Use a blunt-point tapestry needle (see page 143) that has an eye large enough for a single strand of yarn, but will not puncture the sweater fabric or fibers.

1. Backstitch the sweater together either very close to the edges, or wider to fit.

2. Trim the wider seam allowances.

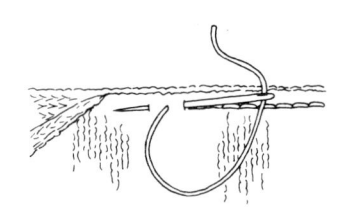

3. Hand overcast with matching thread to prevent raveling.

WOVEN SEAMS

The most invisible seams are woven. Fitting alterations cannot be made along these seams, so reserve this technique for sweaters that fit perfectly.

Stitch to stitch

Used primarily for sweater side seams and armscye areas. Catch the head of the end stitch in a row on each edge alternately, working back and forth.

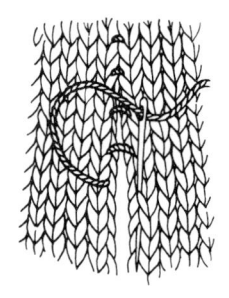

Row to row

Used primarily on shoulder and yoke seams. Put the needle through the stitch on one side. Working in the same direction, put the needle through the stitch on the other side.

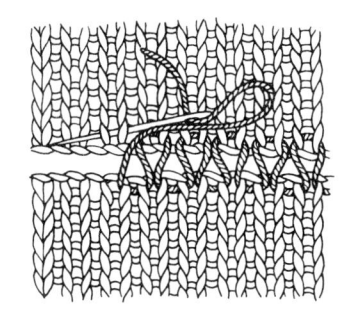

✂. ASSEMBLING BY MACHINE

The quickest assembly method is by machine. Only the laciest openwork cannot be seamed together by machine. Besides being far less time-consuming, this method produces more professional-looking, smoother-fitting sweaters that are durable too. (See Sweater Seams, page 53.)

Using matching thread, sew the sweater together by machine along the marked fitting baste lines.

Ease plus (see page 52) and a roller, even feed, or walking foot prevents seam stretch. Trim excess seam allowance to the stitching.

T-SWEATER TO CROCHET OR KNIT TO FIT

This sweater, shaped like a T, is great for learning the crochet and knit to fit basics. It's simply a combination of rectangular shapes.

Select your yarn and establish the stitch gauge. Make any fitting adjustments on the T-sweater pattern (see page 38).

Crochet or knit to fit and assemble. Add crochet edgings to keep the edges from curling (see page 120). You can add fringe to the shoulder, yoke, and hems (see page 122).

KNIT YOUR OWN RIBBING

After you've caught the sweater craft bug, you'll want to sew more and more sweaters. When it comes to trimming your sweaters, it's not always possible to find ribbing coordinated in color and weight to your sweater fabric.

One solution is to knit your own ribbing. Hand-knitted ribbing is great for cuffs and collars on fur and leather jackets, extra-

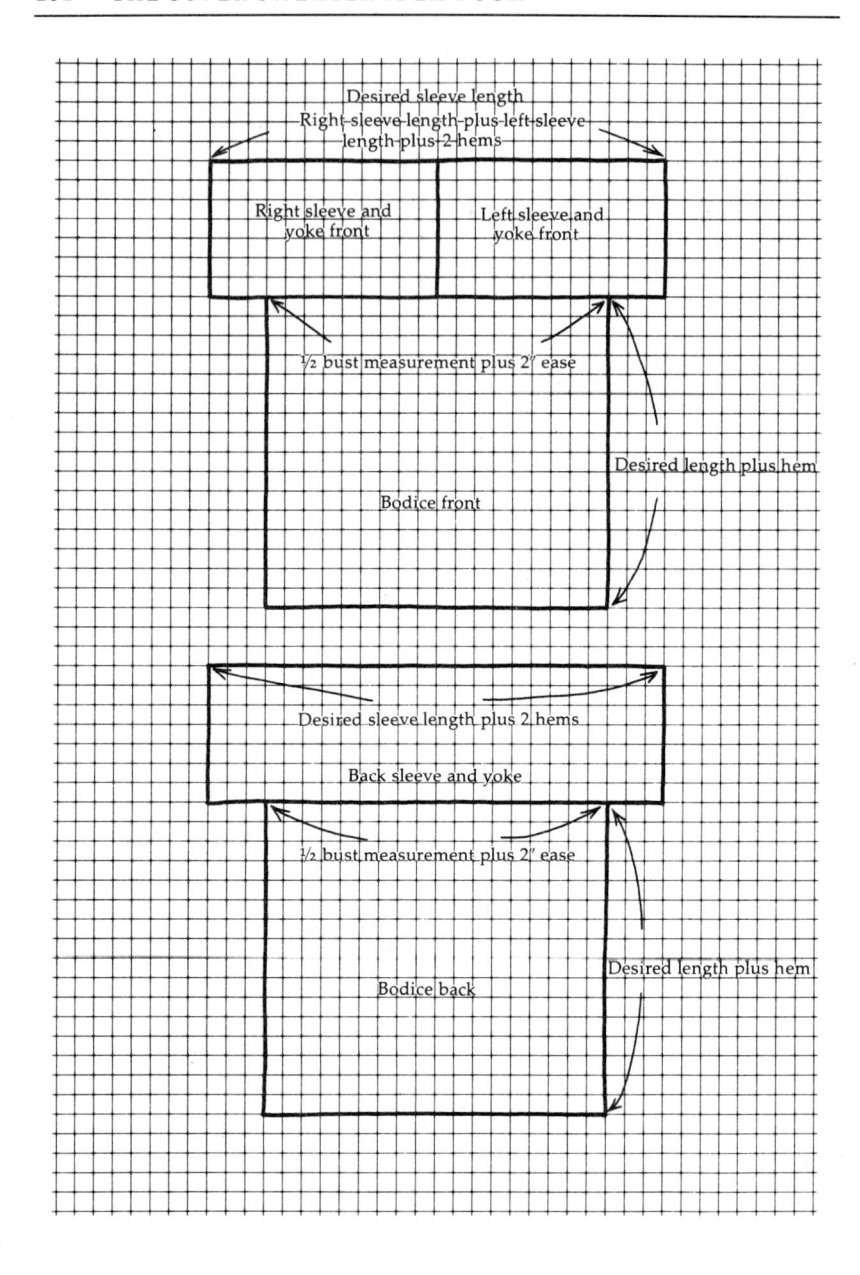

T-Sweater to Crochet or Knit to Fit

heavy sweater knits, etc. (See Sweaters Plus Leather or Fur, page 128.)

Use a yarn weight and needle size that produce a stretchable ribbing lighter in weight than the garment fabric.

1. Cast on just enough stitches so that when you knit, the ribbing will be slightly smaller than the body measurement and will hug figure contours.
2. Knit and purl alternately. A knit 2, purl 2 stitch pattern is most common, although you might want to experiment with different stitch combinations, like knit 3, purl 2. Continue in this pattern to the desired ribbing depth.
3. Cast off.

- For extra firmness and strength, knit the ribbing twice the pattern-determined depth. Fold in half and apply double on the garment.
- If you miscalculate and knit the ribbing too long, simply adjust the fit in the seams that intersect at inconspicuous areas, like underarms, sides, and shoulders. Apply to garment by hand (see page 89) or by machine (see page 53). Trim excess seam allowances.

KNITTING AND CROCHETING ON THE BIAS

If you are hand-knitting or crocheting your sweater fabric, you can create the bias look in the stitch pattern.

KNITTING (STOCKINETTE STITCH)

Cast on the specified or determined number of stitches.

Row 1. Increase 1 stitch in the first stitch. Knit to the last 3 stitches. Knit the next 2 stitches together. Work the last stitch.

Row 2. Purl all stitches. Repeat these two rows for desired length.

Hand-knit bias trim for an unusual sweater finish.

◥. CROCHETING (SINGLE CROCHET)

Chain the specified or determined number of stitches.

Row 1. Single crochet in the 2nd chain from the hook *, chain 1, skip next chain, single crochet in next chain, and repeat from * across. Chain 1, turn.

Row 2. Single crochet, chain 1 and single crochet in the first single crochet stitch, chain 1 *, single crochet in chain 1 space, repeat from * across. Chain 1, turn.

Row 3. Single crochet in first chain 1 space, chain 1 *, single crochet in next chain 1 space, repeat from * across. Chain 1, turn.

Row 4. Repeat Row 2.
Row 5. Repeat Row 3.
Row 6. Repeat Row 2. Alternate Rows 3 and 2 until piece measures the desired length.

Crochet bias trim for sweaters, scarves, trims, or hat and sleeve cuffs. It's an easy stitch pattern that makes ordinary sweaters and accessories your designer originals!

WOVEN HALF SKIRT FOR BULKY KNITS

If your handmade sweater fabric is extremely heavy and bulky, you can add a lightweight woven half skirt cut to fit the waistline and upper hipline areas. *Note:* The finished skirt can only be worn with an overblouse.

1. Knit or crochet from the bottom hem to within 6"–7" of the waistline. Finish off.

2. Choose a skirt pattern (for wovens) that fits you well. Trim it off approximately 7" below the waistline, or just long enough to be covered by an overblouse.

3. Cut out a half skirt using this pattern and matching lightweight woven fabric.

4. Finish the waistline with a conventional waistband and zipper for a close fit making sure you distribute the sweater skirt ease on the woven piece for a smooth fit.

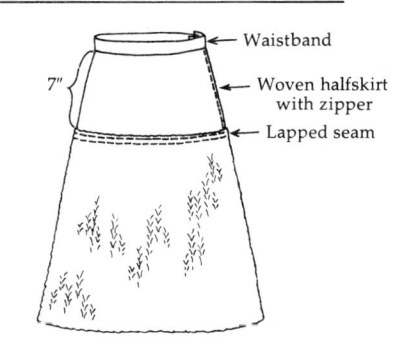

5. Sew the lining half skirt to the sweater fabric, by hand or machine. Lap this seam to minimize bulk.

6. Try on the garment to make sure the stitching doesn't restrict the skirt's hipline ease. Stitch again for reinforcement.

KNIT SPOOL CORDING

Children have learned knitting basics on these spools for years. Once homemade from empty wooden thread spools and nails, today these spools come in plastic with spool hooks, and are available in needlecraft stores. For kids, spool knitting is still a great introduction to sweater craft.

Use the knitted spool cording for belts and ties, worn either singly or several strands together. This knitted tubing is a sure color match for hand-knitted or crocheted garments. Hand sew the cording on your own designs for pillows, afghans, accessories, and monograms. This knitted cording makes drawstrings, curtain ties, and even jewelry. Blind stitch knitted tubing together to make placemats, appliqués, and potholders.

1. Pull end of yarn through the hole in the knitting spool. Leave a 4" yarn extension.
2. Loop yarn around pegs in a crisscross pattern, in a clockwise circular direction.
3. Hold the spool in one hand and the spool hook in the other. Working in the same clockwise direction, pass the yarn around the next peg. Pick up loop on that peg and slip it over the yarn and off the peg.
4. Take stitches off the pegs on the left side. Eventually the knitted cording emerges from the bottom hole of the knitting spool.
5. Continue knitting until the desired length can be measured from the spool top.
6. To cast off, hold the spool with a peg directly in front of you. Take the last stitch off its peg and place it on a peg to the left of it. Drop the bottom stitch over it. Proceed until there is only one loop remaining.
7. Cut the yarn and slip it through the last loop.

Let kids have fun finding their own uses for these stretchable tubings; the tubings are just about unbreakable!

CHAPTER 6

NEW SWEATERS FROM OLD: RECYCLING AND RESTYLING

Here's an opportunity for your design imagination to run wild! You can update old favorite sweaters with embroidery and appliqué. You can recycle parts of old sweaters to make great-looking new ones. Have fun, and don't forget to save the scraps for patchwork.

BORROWED RIBBING

You have sweater fabric, but no ribbing? Borrow ribbing/trim from recyclable sweaters! Search your closets and drawers for old sweaters. Or take a small swatch of your sweater fabric to local thrift stores. Chances are, one of these oldies but goodies will be ribbed and that the ribbing will be the least worn of the entire sweater.

Look for cuff, collar, sleeve, hipline, and neckline ribbing: you'll discover a number of recyclable ribbing possibilities. To ensure cleanliness and colorfastness, pre-launder or dry clean all thrift shop specials before sewing.

Possibilities for ribbing borrowed from recyclables are unlimited. Here are just a few ideas: neckline finishes, cuffs, hat bands, sleeve finishes.

Match the recyclables to your sweater fabric according to color, weight, and stretchability. Ribbings must be elastic to stretch to figure contours.

When the fiber content of the recycled ribbing and the sweater fabric is the same, color coordination will be closer, i.e., acrylic with acrylic, wool with wool, etc. Match the fabric to the ribbing under bright natural light. Also consider laundering requirements. Both the ribbing/trim and the sweater fabric should require similar care.

✎. RECYCLED RIBBED CUFFS

You can cut off the ribbed cuffs from a recyclable sweater and use them on a new one.

1. For sweater with ribbed cuff sewn on, take out seam stitching. For sweater with ribbed cuff knitted in, cut off, leaving a 5/8" seam allowance at the top of the cuff.

2. Try on the cuffs. They should slip on without pulling, yet fit the wrist snugly. If necessary, pin the cuffs to fit, then seam and trim.

3. Double check the sleeve length of the garment. The cuff depth plus the garment sleeve plus ease should equal the finished sleeve length.

4. Divide both the cuffs and the garment sleeves into quarter sections. Mark with pins at these quarter marks. Pin the cuff to the sleeve, right sides together, placing the cuff seam at the sleeve underarm and matching all quarter marks.

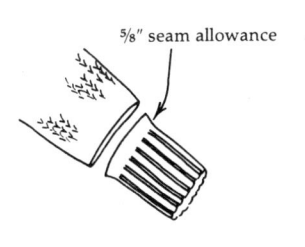

5. With the ribbed cuff on top, sew cuff to the garment sleeve, stretching the ribbing to match all the quarter marks.

Violà! A borrowed cuff that fits and looks custom-made!

NEW LIFE FOR A THRIFT SHOP SPECIAL

Sections of the bias-cut sweater dress shown in the illustration were once parts of a recyclable sweater. The dress needed ribbing for cuffs and the V neckline. We found a man's leisure sweater at a thrift bazaar for only $1.50. It matched the dress fabric perfectly in color, weight, and stretchability. Here's how to do it.

1. The cable stitch section of the sweater becomes the neckline edging of the dress. Cut out cable section leaving 5/8" seam allowances along both long edges.

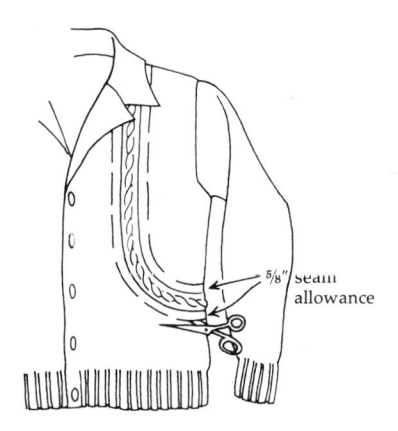

2. Reshape the dress neckline slightly to align with the curve of the new edging piece.

• Most recyclable neckline and cuff ribbing pieces are straight so reshaping is seldom necessary.

3. Miter the center front to fit the dress V (see page 67).

4. Sew the edging section to the dress like a facing: sew a ⅝" seam around the neck edge having right side of ribbing to wrong side of dress.

5. Trim and layer neckline seam to eliminate bulk.

6. Turn the ribbing to the right side of the dress. Turn under ⅝" on the unsewn edge for a hem. Blind stitch.

BIAS TUBE BELT

We made a bias tube belt from the rest of the same thrift shop special.

1. Cut bias strips 2¾" wide from the sweater back.

2. Piece them diagonally into a 60" length.

3. Fold the long bias strip in half lengthwise, right sides together. Sew a ⅝" seam along the three edges, leaving a 2" opening in the center for turning.

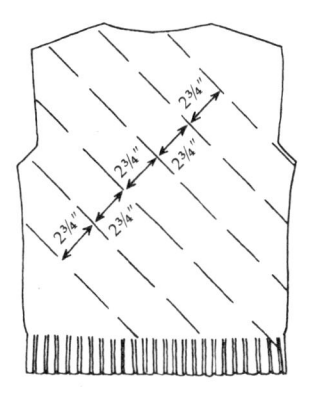

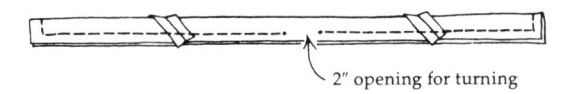

2" opening for turning

4. Turn the belt leaving the seam allowances untrimmed. The extra fabric helps to stuff the tube.

5. Knot the belt ends so they'll hang straight during wear. Save scraps of recycled sweaters for other sweater craft projects. You can make toys and patchwork items from small fabric pieces.

PATCHWORK SWEATER CRAFT PROJECTS

If you have saved old sweaters for patchwork, you can combine colors and textures that blend to make new sweater garments, accessories, and home furnishings.

Pre-launder all sweaters before cutting into patches.

1. Cut the sweater patches along the lengthwise rib and crosswise course to form squares and rectangles of the desired size.

2. Sew the sweater patches together by hand or by machine. You can work blanket stitch and/or single crochet (see pages 118 and 155) around the patches for a decorative effect and to prevent raveling. (See page 117 for edge finishes.)

3. After you make sweater fabric from the patches, lay out the pattern, cut, and sew.

Sweater pillows, quilts, and bedspreads can be pieced together to size. (See page 199 for other home accessory ideas.) Full-size throw bedspreads are simply large rectangles, hemmed along all four edges. Although you should measure beds for a proper fit, there are standard measurements. Remember to add in hem, seam, and tuck-in allowances.

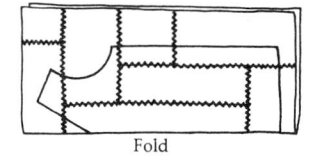

Fold

STANDARD BED MEASUREMENTS
(Measurements in inches)

	Bedspreads Width × Length	Comforters/ Quilts Width × Length
Twin	81 × 115	72 × 90
Full (Double)	96 × 118	80 × 90
Queen	102 × 120	108 × 90
King	114 × 120	108 × 90

NEW PILLOWS FROM OLD SWEATERS

Somewhere in your closets and drawers you must have some old, perhaps only partially worn out sweaters that deserve renewed consideration. Or maybe you've come across a

New Sweaters from Old: Recycling and Restyling • 173

worn but good-looking sweater in a thrift shop. If you don't recycle them as garments, how about using them as home furnishings?

A wool patchwork sweater from a thrift shop had colors perfect for a living room—earthy tones of beige, gray, camel, and orange. Part of the inspiration to make a pillow out of it came from the sweater colors and the patchwork design. To take advantage of the patchwork pattern, we cut an oval shape out of the center of the sweater. Let the unique pattern and colors *you* find inspire your design imagination. You'll discover shortcuts and construction ideas that work for your particular sweater project.

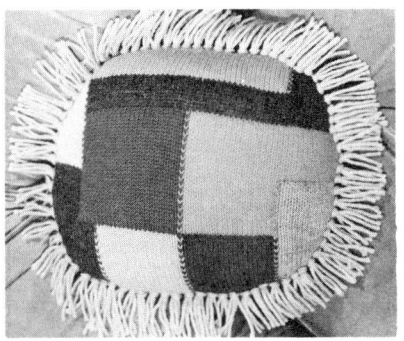

Here's how to make a pillow from a patchwork sweater. (See Sweater Pillows, page 200, for complete pillow-making instructions.)

1. Cut out the pillow front from the sweater. Fold this front piece in half to use as a pattern for the back.
2. Double a piece of matching woven fabric for the pillow back. Use the folded pillow front as a pattern, but add ⅝" seam allowances to the center folded edge for the zipper.
3. To accent the patchwork, quilt the sweater fabric before sewing it to the back side: sandwich a layer of fiberfill between the sweater fabric and a corresponding piece of nonwoven interfacing. Then outline the patchwork designs with straight machine stitching (6–8 stitches per inch), creating a puffy quilted effect.

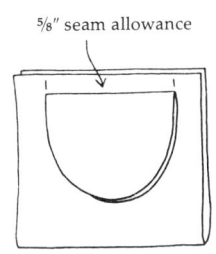

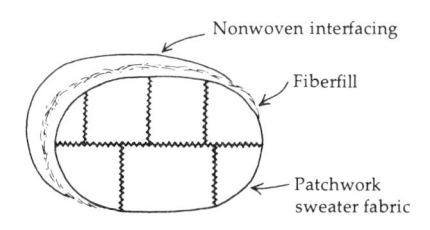

⅝" seam allowance

Nonwoven interfacing
Fiberfill
Patchwork sweater fabric

4. Sew a 6" zipper in the middle of the back pillow piece.

5. Make an inner pillow form casing in the same oval shape (use the pillow as a pattern).

6. Sew the front and back pillow pieces together, right sides together.

7. Turn right sides out through the zipper opening.

8. Place the inner form inside the pillow and stuff.

9. If you wish, add a 4" fringe along the finished edge of the oval pillow to highlight one of the patchwork colors and make the pillow seem larger.

SWEATER FACE-LIFTS

Have any sweaters hidden in the back of your closets or drawers that could use a face-lift? In one evening you can transform those "never wears" into wearable favorites with iron-on embroidery transfers and a few simple stitches or decorative appliqués. Surprise someone special with a "new" sweater made from a "golden oldie."

IRON-ON EMBROIDERY TRANSFERS

Iron-on transfers are obtainable through most pattern companies and some are made specifically for sweaters!

The sweaters can be ready-to-wear or home-sewn garments that have been knitted in a relatively flat stitch like stockinette. Sweaters knitted in lacy or cable stitches do not accept the iron-on transfer completely and make difficult working surfaces for the embroidery.

• Before you iron on the transfer, wash the sweater to remove any sizing or soil that could hamper the design transfer process.

• Test the iron-on transfer (testing samples are usually provided) on an inside corner of the sweater. Is there any running and smearing? If so, use another sweater for this project.

• Choose embroidery yarn that corresponds as closely as possible in weight and thickness to the yarn used in the sweater. For example, use a sport-weight yarn when you embroider a lightweight sweater or use a knitting worsted weight on a heavy or bulky sweater.

1. Cut out the transfer design leaving enough paper around design for pinning. Place the printed side of the transfer down and pin to the right side of the sweater. The transfer cannot be removed after it is ironed on, so position the design carefully.

2. Set dry iron at correct fabric temperature. If in doubt about the fabric, use wool setting. Press the iron firmly over the entire transfer, completely lifting the iron in an up-and-down motion. Do not slide the iron across the transfer because this will create a blurred outline. *Caution:* Do not stretch the sweater fabric while pressing.

3. Remove a few pins to check the impression: if the transfer is not sharp, continue to press over the paper until a clear impression is obtained. Before the transfer cools, remove the paper.

4. Allow the transfer impression to cool and dry completely before embroidering over the design lines.

✎. STITCH, STUFF, AND PUFF APPLIQUÉS

Make any old sweater look like a new sweater with this appliquéd trapunto technique. It's also an easy way to coordinate a sweater with a woven skirt or dress. Best of all, it's an instant success sweater craft idea for beginning sewers!

1. Draw or trace the appliqué design on paper. Appliqué designs can follow fabric print outlines such as flowers and figures.

2. Cut the appliqué out of the fashion fabric. Use a woven fabric that does not ravel excessively or a firm knit. If necessary, stabilize the appliqué

with lightweight fusible interfacing, on the wrong side.

On lighter weight or stretchable fabrics, back the area to be appliquéd with lightweight fusible interfacing. (Test a small swatch of the interfacing on the wrong side of the sweater fabric before applying.)

3. Stitch directionally around the appliqué design (use a narrow, close zig-zag stitch or 12–15 per inch straight stitches).

4. Leave a 1" opening to "stuff and puff" with polyester fiberfill. Close the opening with stitching.

5. Stitch over any other appliqué design lines. A 3-D trapunto effect is the result.

Once you see how simple this method is, you'll want to use "stitch, stuff, and puff" appliqués on children's sweaters, toys, home furnishings, and sweater craft projects of all kinds!

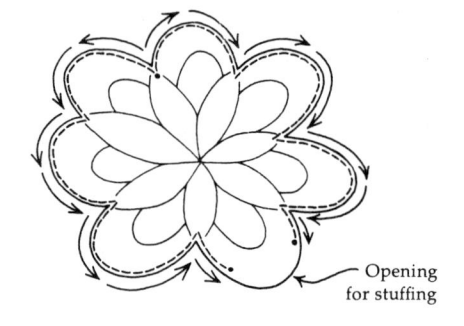

Opening for stuffing

✂. FREE MACHINE EMBROIDERY

Machine embroidery is great for jazzing up a plain sweater or camouflaging worn spots and holes. The technique requires some sewing expertise and practice, yet after you master the method, you can create original designs easily.

Back the sweater fabric with lightweight fusible interfacing to prevent the design area from stretching. Test the stitch and the interfacing on a sample swatch of sweater fabric first. On some lightweight sweater knits, machine embroidery is too heavy and will cause stretching and puckering.

1. Draw the design on tracing paper (a continuous line makes sewing easier).

2. Put the interfaced sweater area to be embroidered in an embroidery hoop. Pin the design pattern on the sweater fabric.

3. Sew the outline with a straight stitch or a narrow zig-zag. Remove the paper.

4. Lower the machine feed dogs so that *you* can control fabric movement. Set your stitch length at 0. *Remove the presser foot.* Lower the presser bar to give tension to the upper thread.

5. Move the hoop to form a zig-zag stitch over the first stitching line around the design, covering the stitching completely. Move the work slowly so that the stitches are close together, creating the embroidery effect.

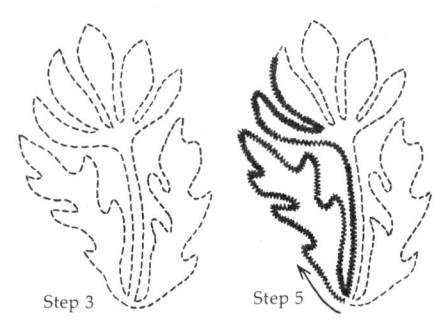

You can sew entire scenes, using this machine embroidery technique.

RESTYLING HANDMADES

It's a shame to throw handmades away especially since someone at some time spent many hours creating the now outdated garment. It's nicer—and more practical—to restyle them instead. Here's one possibility.

Crocheted or knitted dresses that are too short can be shortened to tunic or blouse length.

1. On the old garment carefully cut along a row line. One or two rows may have to be raveled off to even up the hem edge.
2. Secure the edge and reinforce intersecting seams with machine or hand stitching using matching thread.
3. If the garment edge needs finishing, work a row of single crochet (see page 155) into the fabric. You might have to prepare the fabric edge for finishing (see page 121). Coordinate the look by finishing the hem, neckline, cuffs, or armholes, with the same yarn.

MENDING SWEATERS

There was a time when individuals had to spend many hours in front of the fireplace darning socks and sweaters. But today's time-conscious home sewers have a choice—to mend by hand or by machine—since modern sewing machines are equipped to do this kind of sewing. Mending by machine is a much quicker process.

On some sweaters you could embroider (see page 174) or appliqué (see page 175) to disguise small sweater holes instead of darning.

DARN IT—BY MACHINE

All you need for darning by machine are a zig-zag sewing machine (a free arm machine is helpful for darning socks and sweater sleeves), a darning foot (see machine manual for description of this foot attachment), matching thread, and lightweight yarn.

1. Lower the feed dogs. Set stitch width and length to 0: *you will be moving the sweater fabric under the foot, determining the stitch length.* Refer to the machine manual for darning settings and procedures.
2. Change to the darning foot. Thread the machine with matching thread. Only on very heavy sweaters should heavier thread, topstitching, or darning thread be used because these threads make the mending too bulky.
3. Place the sweater or sock hole over the lowered feed dogs and under the darning foot. Fasten a strand of the matching yarn on one side of the hole with a few machine stitches. Working from left to right, fill the hole with the yarn, catching it with machine stitching on both sides.

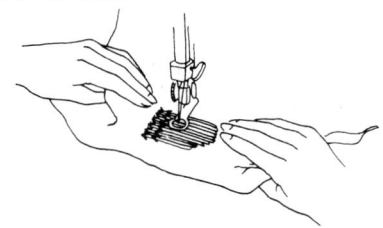

4. After the hole has been covered with yarn, zig-zag back and forth over the strands at a slow speed to darn mend.

• If the zig-zag stitches are placed too close together, the darning becomes too stiff and uncomfortable.

✎. DARNING BY HAND

1. Steam press the worn area of the sweater. Clip any damaged stitches away from the hole, so you'll have a straight line to follow.

2. Using matching yarn of similar weight, run the yarn back and forth, filling the hole.

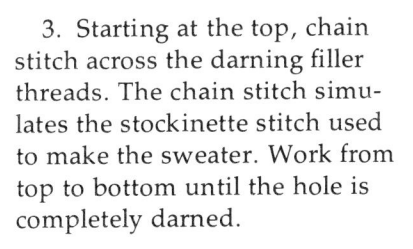

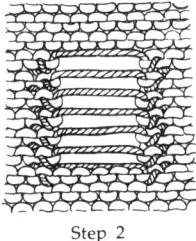

3. Starting at the top, chain stitch across the darning filler threads. The chain stitch simulates the stockinette stitch used to make the sweater. Work from top to bottom until the hole is completely darned.

Step 2

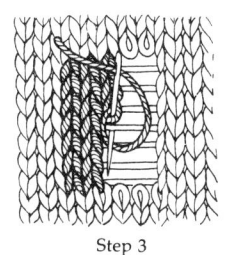

Step 3

THINNING AREAS

On heavier sweaters that have worn areas, reinforce with a strand of matching yarn worked in and out of the stitch pattern on the wrong side. This method is great for thinning elbow areas.

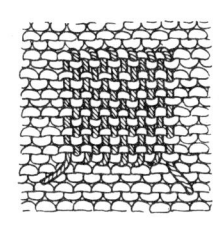

✎. LEATHER PATCHING

Leather patches, both real and imitation, are inexpensive and readily available in most variety, fabric, and department stores.

Leather patches cover up and protect worn areas on sweater craft garments, especially elbows on long sleeve sweaters.

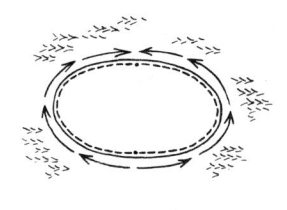

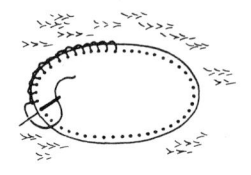

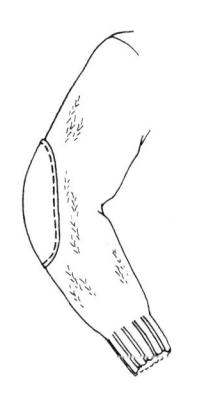

1. Before applying the patches, darn the sweater by machine (faster!) or by hand.
2. Pin or tape the patches in place.
3. Using a straight or zig-zag stitch, sew the patches to the sweater, directionally.

• A free arm sewing machine is helpful when you're applying the patches to tubular areas like sleeves and pant legs.

Or sew the patches on by hand with a blanket stitch worked through pre-punched holes (see page 129).

When you mend children's clothes, you can cut the leather into shapes children would enjoy, like animals or cars.

CHAPTER **7**

MUCH MORE THAN SWEATERS

There are so many things to make with sweater craft, and lots of them are not sweaters at all! You can make toys for children, items for your home, accessories for everyone. What they all have in common is sweater fabric and easy construction. Most of the projects in this chapter can be completed in an evening. They're useful, good-looking, and make great gifts!

WARM AND COSY ACCESSORIES

↙. HOODED SWEATER SCARF

One simple seam transforms this long strip of sweater fabric into a hooded scarf. This practical scarf doubles as a carry-all because the deep hems on both ends are pockets!

Materials

Sweater fabric: ¾ yd., 54"–72" wide, of medium to heavyweight fabric. Or if you knit or crochet the fabric, make a piece 13" × 88". For lighter-weight fabrics, cut the scarf double width. You need twice as much fabric (1½ yds.).

Yarn: Optional for fringe trim.

1. Cut two 46" × 13" strips.
2. Seam along the 13" sides, right sides together.

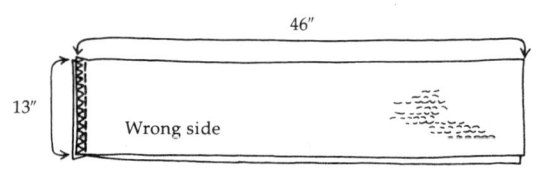

3. Turn up 2" on each end of the scarf to form pocket top. Secure with machine stitching, fusible adhesive, decorative handstitching, or hand hemstitch.

- This step is not necessary if you crochet or knit your fabric because of the finished edge.

4. Turn up the scarf ends another 6" to form the pocket. Baste in place.

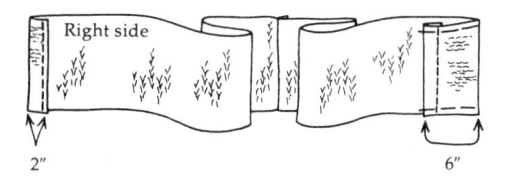

Much More than Sweaters • 183

5. Fold the scarf in half right sides together. Sew from the top seam 10" down one side, forming the hood. A narrow seam can be used, ¼"–½".

6. Finish all scarf edges. Ends can be fringed (see page 122) and the edges can be blanket stitched and/or worked in single crochet (see pages 118 and 155).

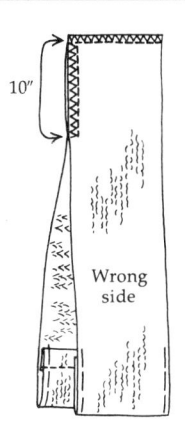

↙. TUBE HAT AND SCARF

You'll be surprised how easy tube hats and scarves are to make. When you want to make more than one hat or scarf, choose the tube style: they're fast, fun, and fit great!

Materials for tube hat (adult size)

Sweater fabric: ¾ yd., or any sweater fabric piece 26" × 16". Choose a very stretchable sweater fabric.

Yarn: Optional, for pom-pom, 4 oz. skein of knitting worsted.

1. Cut out the sweater fabric to a 16" wide (with the crosswise stretch) and 26" long size. You might have to alter the width dimension slightly to fit very large or small head sizes, or to compensate for stretchability differences. To check the fit, stretch the fabric around the head. Mark the width to size (not too tight!)

2. Stitch the tube, right sides together, along the 26" side. Be careful not to stretch this edge while stitching—ease plus helps (see page 52). Trim excess seam allowances.

3. Turn the tube right side out. Fold in half wrong sides together.

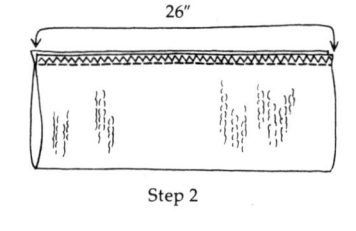

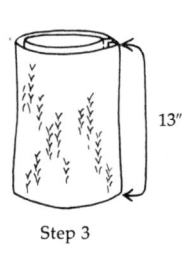

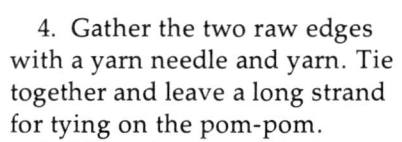

Step 2

Step 3

Step 4

4. Gather the two raw edges with a yarn needle and yarn. Tie together and leave a long strand for tying on the pom-pom.

5. Make the pom-pom (see page 125). Sew on to the hat. Bring all loose yarn strands to the inside of the hat and tie off.

6. Try on the tube hat. Adjust the cuff depth.

Materials for tube scarf

Sweater fabric: ¾ yd., 54"–72" wide. This fabric doesn't have to be as stretchable as that used for the tube hat. (It can be moderately stretchable.) It should be soft for comfortable neck wear.

1. Cut ¾ yd. of sweater fabric. Straighten the crosswise course on both edges (see page 40). The crosswise grain runs the length of the scarf, the lengthwise grain runs the width. The grain directions can be switched, but then the scarf would require twice as much fabric.

2. Fold the fabric in half along the crosswise grain, right sides together. Stitch along the long edge with a sweater seam—ease plus helps to prevent stretching of these edges (see pages 52 and 53). Trim any excess seam allowances.

3. Turn right side out. Gather both ends of the scarf with yarn to form the tube. Make and attach pom-poms (see page 125).

✂. NECK AND WRIST WARMERS

These two items make great gifts for skiers, skaters, hunters, and other outdoor people! Neck and wrist warmers sewn from old sweaters are easy to make and fun to give, and they help fight off winter chills.

Wool or wool blends are extra durable and warm. Styles can vary, but turtlenecks are best for neck warmers.

Materials for neck warmer

One turtleneck sweater: Don't choose wool if the wearer has an allergic reaction.

Simply trim the sweater off at the turtleneck seam. With matching thread, finish raw edge with a zig-zag stitch, machine overlock, or hand whipstitch. Do not stretch the edge while stitching.

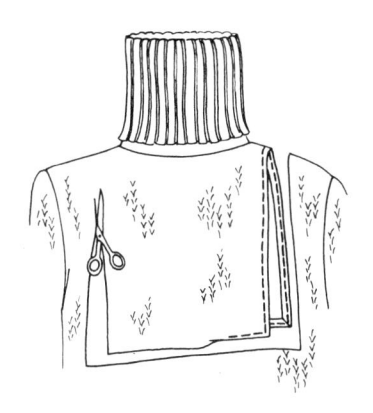

If a dickey style is preferred, trim the sweater as shown, front and back. Don't throw away the rest of the sweater—save the ribbing for wrist warmers and matching head bands.

Turn under dickey raw edges ½" and machine stitch in place. On bulky sweater knits, hand overcast the raw edge with matching yarn.

Materials for wrist warmer

One sweater with 2"–4" sleeve and bottom ribbed edge. You can match this to the neck warmer for a gift set. Choose a knit and fiber that won't stretch out easily.

1. Cut sleeve ribbing from the sweater, leaving ⅝" for seam allowances. Open ribbing along the seam to reduce bulk.
2. Using this flat, rectangular sleeve ribbing as a pattern, cut two corresponding pieces of ribbing from the sweater bottom. (You should have four ribbing pieces, two cut from the sleeves and two from the hem.)
- Instead of using the sweater bottom ribbing, you can cut ribbing from another sweater sleeve in a matching or contrasting color.
3. Seam two ribbing pieces right sides together along the ⅝" seam allowance raw edge with a zig-zag, stretch, or straight stitch (see Sweater Seams, page 53). Ease plus this seam (see page 52).
4. Fit the ribbed band to the wrist; pin baste for a snug fit. Stitch from each finished edge toward the center along the pin baste markings. Clip threads.

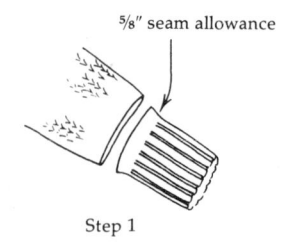

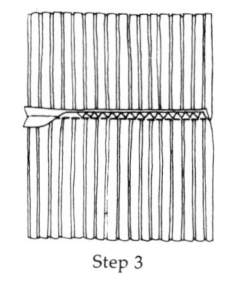

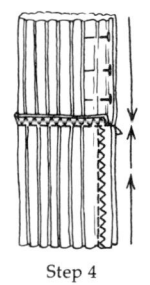

COLD WEATHER HEADBAND

Another cold weather accessory that can be made from old sweaters is a ribbed headband. You can match or coordinate this headband to the neck and wrist warmers.

Materials

One sweater that's very elastic, but not too bulky.

1. Cut the bottom ribbing off the sweater. You need a piece at least 4" × 12".
2. To finish the one raw edge, turn under ½" and machine stitch ¼" from the fold.
- For lightweight sweater fabrics, use a double layer of fabric. Sew the long seams with right sides together. Turn. Follow Steps 3 and 4.
3. Stretch the headband strip around the wearer's head until it is snug but comfortable. Mark the seam placement.
4. Stitch the headband seam, right sides together. Turn right sides out.

➤ SWEATER KNIT BOOT TOPPERS

Boot toppers are all the rage, and they double as leg warmers too. They're expensive to buy, but they cost almost nothing to make at home. You probably won't have to buy any fabric: use scraps from sweater craft projects or check closets for dust-collecting sweaters. It's also a super quick gift idea (make them easily in an hour) for boot wearers. One size fits all.

Materials

An old sweater, sweater body, or sweater fabric by the yard: Any large enough to cut two 8½" × 22" pieces. (Stretch should run along the 8½" side, or around the leg.)

Nonroll elastic: ½ yd. of 1"–1½" wide.

1. Fold the piece of sweater knit in half, right sides together. Stitch a ⅝" sweater seam (see page 53). Be careful not to stretch this seam as you stitch. Trim excess seam allowances.

2. Turn down a 6" cuff, wrong side to wrong side, on one end of the topper. Straight stitch ⅜" from the raw edge, through both thicknesses to hold the cuff in place.

3. Use ease plus to finish the other raw edge with a zig-zag, overlock, or hand whipstitch. Do not stretch the edge while sewing. (See page 52.) This edge will be inside the boot, so it doesn't need to be hemmed.

4. Mark the toppers with pins at quarter intervals. The long seam should be positioned at the back of the leg.

5. Sew 7½" of elastic to the side quarter marks, placing approximately ⅜" on the wrong side.

6. Fold the top cuff in half (3") toward the right side. Your boot toppers are done!

For small children or big men, the length and width of these boot toppers will have to be altered. Measure the boot length and calf circumference and adjust topper size accordingly. Be sure to take the sweater knit stretch into account (see Commercial Pattern Stretch Gauge, page 19).

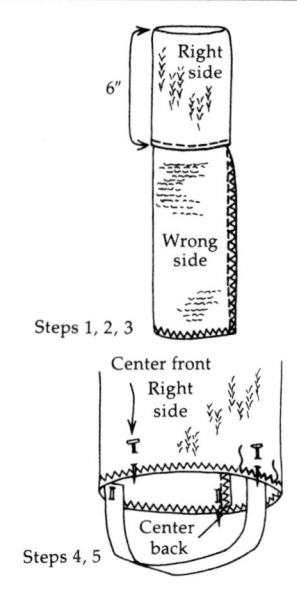

MORE ACCESSORY IDEAS

◣. SWEATER CRAFT PURSE

This purse has a real heirloom look and it doesn't take ages to make (you can complete it in an hour)! Carry your yarn and needlecraft projects in this easy-to-make purse. Customize it with fringe, crochet trim, embroidery accents, or contrasting lining.

Materials

Sweater fabric: ¾ yd., 45"–60" wide. Can be purchased by the yard or knitted/crocheted to fit purse pattern dimensions (see Crochet or Knit to Fit, page 148). Choose fabric stable enough to retain the purse shape.

Lining: ¾ yd., 36"–45" wide. Optional, depending on the type of sweater knit used. Recommended to prevent see-through, fall-out, or bagging.

Purse handles: Can be purchased or borrowed from old

purses—check your closets or thrift and antique shops.

1. Cut out fabric and lining for the two pockets.
- Machine or hand embroidered initials can be added to the pockets before they are sewn to the purse.
2. Finish pocket edges with crochet or embroidery stitches. Topstitch pockets on bag.
3. Mark a point 4½" from the top on the two sides. With right sides together, stitch around side and bottom edges of the purse starting at one mark and ending at the other. Backstitch. Clip to stitching.
4. If you're lining the purse, follow the same procedure for the lining pieces. Put the lining and the sweater purse pieces wrong sides together.
5. On the 4½" extensions, fold back ½" on both sides and topstitch with a straight or zigzag stitch. Don't worry about the raw edges; sweater knits usually don't ravel!
6. To form the casing, turn back the raw edge 1½" and top-

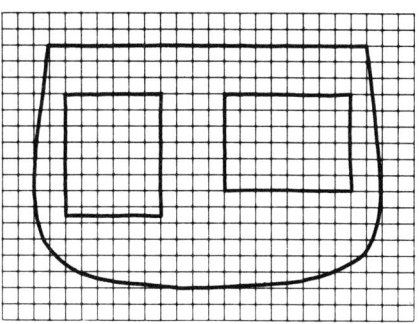

Purse and pockets pattern showing placement
1 square = 1"

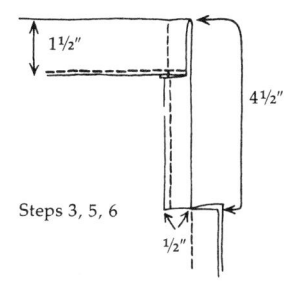

Steps 3, 5, 6

stitch close to the raw edge through all thicknesses.
- If working on "unbroken" purse handles, fold the casing (1") over the bar, then stitch in place. A zipper foot attachment is helpful when sewing a casing over continuous handles.
7. Slide casing onto handle at center opening. Adjust gathers.

GOLF CLUB MITTS

Send your favorite golfer out in style with these golf club mitts. They're made from sweater fabric so they stretch to fit. Sew a matching vest or sweater too. You can make the whole ensemble in less time than it would take to knit or crochet the mitt alone.

These three mitts are designed for the 1, 3, and 4 woods. Of course, you can make more mitts for the other clubs.

Materials

Sweater fabric: ¾ yd. or a sweater body, 30" × 10" (can be recycled). Preferably the fabric should be very stretchable (ribbed is best!). An old sweater can be cut up to make the mitts too. Measure the same dimensions as those specified for the sweater body.

• It's practical to select a washable fabric and yarn: the golf club mitts get soiled during use and need frequent laundering.

Yarn: One 4 oz. skein of knitting worsted in a contrasting color for trim and pom-poms.

1. Cut out the mitts, 10" × 10". If you're using sweater fabric by the yard, double the width (to 20") to make a finished edge.

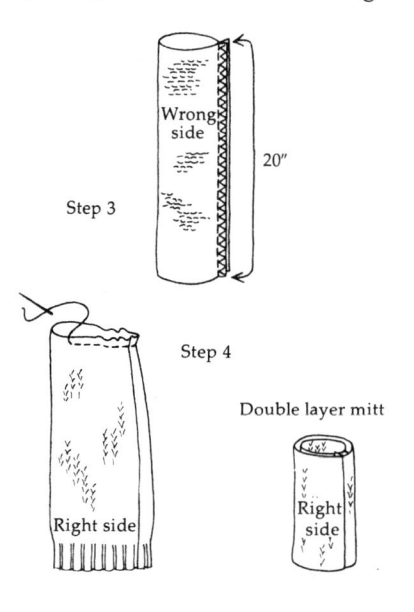

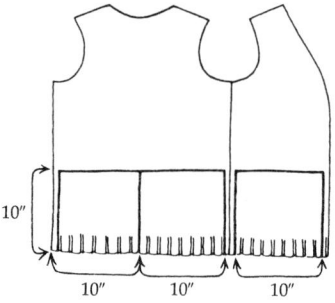

2. Baste the club number ring lines on the mitts.

3. Right sides together, sew the long side (along the lengthwise rib) with a ⅝" sweater seam (see page 53).

4. Turn the mitt right side out. Using a tapestry needle and yarn, gather the raw edge. Leave long tie strands for attaching the pom-pom.

• For double layer mitts, turn right side out after sewing the longer seam. Then fold in half wrong sides together. Draw up both raw edges, leaving long tie strands for attaching the pom-pom.

5. Put a light bulb or tennis ball inside the mitt to stretch the fabric slightly.

6. Chain embroider the club number rings on the mitt with a strand of contrasting color yarn. Follow the basting lines sewn previously. The chain stitching worked on the slightly stretched-out mitt shapes it to fit the club size.

7. Make extra-thick pom-poms to stand up better during use (see page 125).

8. Attach the pom-poms to the mitts with the yarn strands. Tie and knot inside the mitt. Clip the ends.

Sew a matching tube hat and scarf to complete your golfer's accessory set.

SWEATERS ARE FOR KIDS

BABY BLANKET

Keep a baby snug and warm in this blanket or bath wrap. It's a great gift idea!

Materials

Sweater fabric: 2½ yds. of 58"–60". Should be "baby soft" and washable.

Yarn: One 4 oz. skein for trim. Yarn should be similar or lighter in weight than the fabric.

1. Cut two large squares, both 45" × 45", out of the sweater fabric. Round the corners slightly.

2. Place the two large squares together, right sides together.

3. Stitch a ⅝" seam around the blanket, leaving 3"–4" unsewn for turning. Do not stretch the edge while stitching. Trim the excess seam allowance.

4. Turn the blanket to the right side. Hand blind stitch or machine topstitch to close the opening.

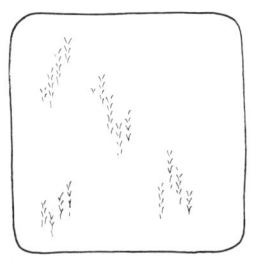

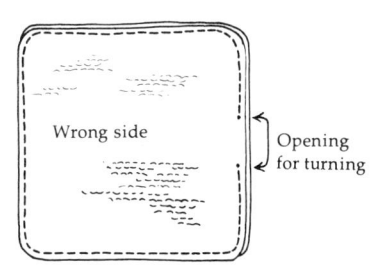

5. Finish the blanket edges with fringe (see page 122), blanket stitch (see page 118), or a row of single crochet (see page 155). Work the crochet into the blanket stitch or directly into larger stitch sweater fabrics.

⌇. THE SOFTEST BABY BONNET

Make this soft bonnet for newborns: it's a quick gift that is a hit at any baby shower.

Materials

Sweater fabric: 12" × 12", very soft, light to medium weight fabric, washable. Look for baby colors—pastels and white. Use sweater fabric by the yard, scraps, or recyclable garments.

Matching yarn: One skein for edge stitching and ties. Yarn should be similar or lighter in weight than the sweater fabric.

1. Fold the square of sweater fabric right sides together. Leave a 1½" extension single layer on one side.
2. Sew the diagonal seam lines, backstitching at each end. Trim the seams. This is the crown of the bonnet.

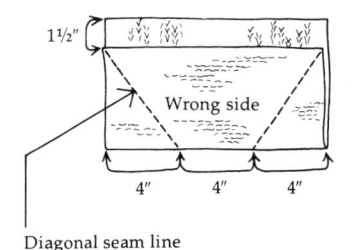

Diagonal seam line

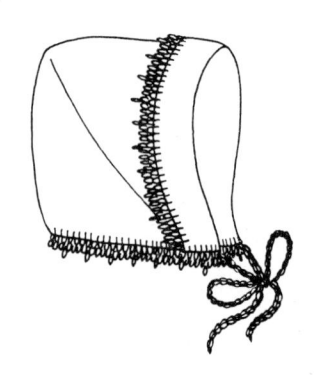

3. Turn the bonnet right side out.
4. Fold back the 1½" extension. Finish the bottom edge and this extension with blanket stitching and single crochet (see page 155).
   - For a special delicate border, work a picot crochet edging in the first stitching row. Work one single crochet in each of the first four stitches. Chain 3. Slipstitch in the last single crochet made. Repeat across the edge.
5. Continue the extension edging in a chain stitch to form the under chin ties (9" each side). For thicker chin ties, work a row of single crochet in the chain stitch.

If you make a matching crib blanket, trim it with the same edging. They'll make a perfect shower gift set.

⌇. MITTENS IN MINUTES

If you've got some little hands in your family that need warming, make a pair of these mittens—in minutes! It's a great gift item.

Materials

Sweater fabric that's warm but not too bulky or too lightweight and is stretchable. Mittens made of stable sweater fabric are uncomfortable. Washable fabrics are best for children. Old sweaters can be recycled to make several pairs of mittens. Sweater bodies are excellent for mittens that fit because of their finished rib edge.

1. To make the mitten pattern, place the hand on a piece of butcher paper or nonwoven interfacing. Trace around the thumb and fingers, allowing 1"–1¼" for wearing ease and seam allowances.

- The length of the mittens is up to you. Don't make them too short or your wearer will have cold wrists!

2. Lay out the mitten pattern on the sweater fabric. The more stretchable fabric grain direction (usually crosswise) should go around the hand. Mittens hug the wrist better if you place the ribbing at the bottom edge.

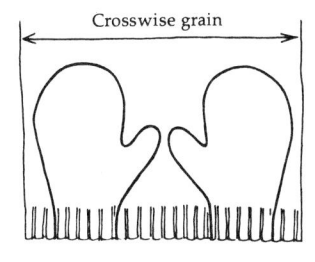

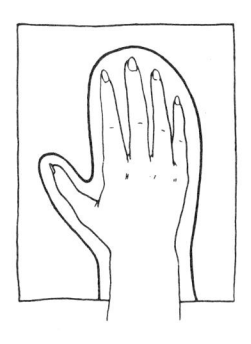

- If the sweater fabric doesn't have a finished rib edge, apply a ribbing band after the mitten is sewn together.

3. Be sure to cut enough mitten pieces: cut two each for the right and left hands.

4. Sew the mitten pieces together with a ⅝" sweater seam right sides together, in the directions shown (see page 53). Use a stretch zig-zag stitch and the ease plus method (see page 52). Be careful not to stretch this seam while sewing. Trim the seam to the stitching.

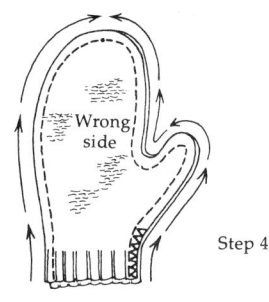

- Very stretchable fabrics can be difficult to sew by machine without stretching. Hand stitch these using matching yarn.

Either sew the mitten together from the wrong side with a whipstitch (see page 117) or, from the right side, blanket stitch the mitten together. Work a single crochet stitch around the mitten edges in the blanket stitching (see pages 118 and 155).

5. If your sweater fabric does not have a finished edge, fit a piece of ribbing to the wearer's wrist: it should fit snugly. Distribute the mitten ease evenly. Then sew to the mitten from the ribbing side. The mittens are made—in minutes!

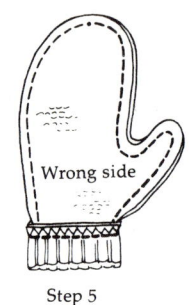

Hand stitching

Step 5

CUSTOM TOUCHES

- Keep mitten pairs together with twisted yarn cording (see page 113) finished with puffy pom-poms (see page 125).

- Work embroidery designs or initials into the mittens with yarn.

IS IT A TOY? NO, IT'S A SWEATER PILLOW IN DISGUISE!

Pillows don't have to be round, rectangular, or square, although most are. Have fun with your pillow shapes. If you make a pillow for children, ask them what the fabric reminds them of . . . a lamb? A bird? A kitty cat? Then cut out the pillow in the whimsical shape of their chosen animal. Keep the shapes simple, with minimal projections like legs and ears, since they're hard to shape and stuff evenly.

➘. CECIL, THE FUNNY-FACED OWL

Cecil's official habitat is a child's room, but he has been known to appear mysteriously on the living room couch or a favorite TV easy chair.

An owl has a very simple shape and is so huggable when made of a soft sweater fabric. Best of all, Cecil can be made from a man's old pullover sweater—leather elbow patches and all.

Materials

Sweater fabric: A recyclable man's pullover sweater, preferably a large size and long style (the owl is 22" long). Or use two old sweaters, and cut the front and back out of the two different fabrics. Or buy ⅔ yd. sweater fabric by the yard.

Velveteen: For soft "feathers," ½ yd. was used for the chest area. Any soft fabric is usable but a napped surface adds to the feather effect.

Leather or leatherlike patches: Two for the owl eyes. Buy a package of leather patches or cut off elbow patches from an old sweater. Suede adds another soft texture to the owl pillow.

Felt scraps: For the eyes.

Matching yarn and thread: For topstitching and fringing, approximately 4 oz. medium to heavy weight yarn.

Polyester fiberfill: 12" × 12" sheet of batting and approximately 2 lb. for pillow stuffing.

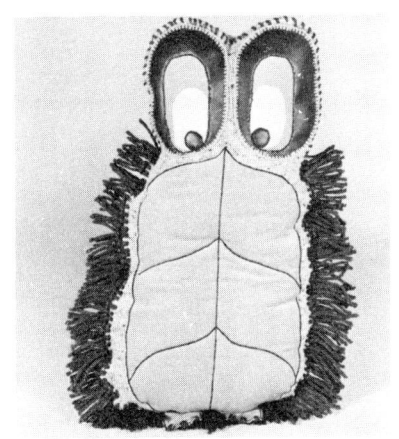

Nonwoven interfacing: ⅔ yd. for inner pillow casing.

1. Cut out all pattern pieces adding ⅝" seam allowances. Cut out the owl body from the sweater front and back. Using the chest piece as a pattern, cut out a thin layer of fiberfill.

2. Cut out inner pillow facing (owl body size) from nonwoven interfacing.

3. Sandwich the fiberfill between the velveteen chest piece and the right side of the front owl section.

4. Topstitch in place with a wide satin stitch along stitching lines, as graphed. If you don't have a zig-zag machine, a straight stitch (6–8 inches per inch) can be substituted. The fiberfill should lift the chest piece between the stitching lines.

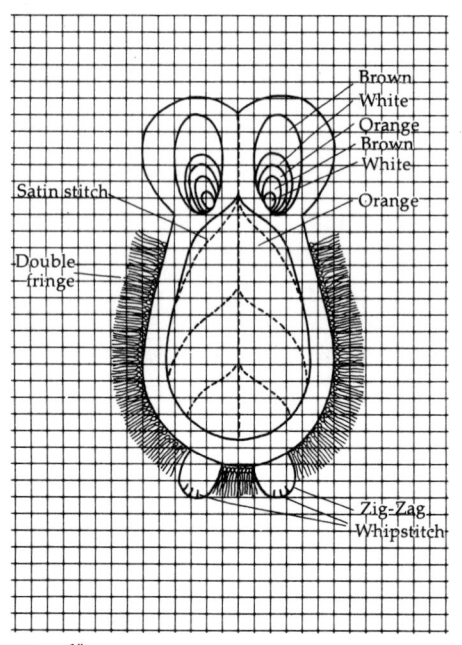

196 • THE SUPER SWEATER IDEA BOOK

1 square = 1″

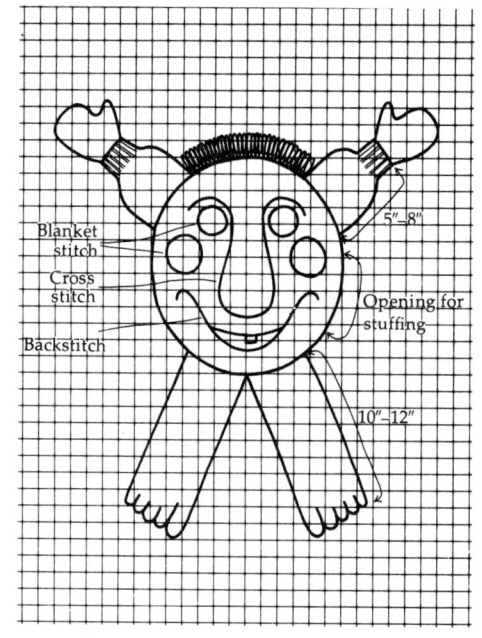

1 square = 1″

5. Tape the eyes in place on the front section. (Don't use pins because they tend to lump the fabric, causing crooked sewing.)

6. Sew on the leather patches by hand with a blanket stitch; pre-punched holes around the edges make it easy (see page 129).

7. Machine stitch the other eye pieces in place. Remove the tape.

8. Sandwich a small amount of fiberfill between the wrong sides of the foot pattern pieces. Satin stitch the edge. Trim to stitching. Pin the owl's feet to the front section.

9. Sew the front section to the back section, leaving a 3"–4" opening along one side for stuffing.

10. Make the pillow inner casing, leaving an opening in the same place along the side as in the outer owl. Put the pillow casing into the pillow. Stuff until Cecil is puffy and filled out but not too hard.

11. Whipstitch the inner casing opening first and then the pillow opening.

12. Finish the pillow edges with double-row fringe approximately 2" long (see page 123).

13. Add claws to the feet by whipstitching in the three spots with yarn.

✧. SUPER SWEATERMAN

You want to make rather than buy a gift for that special little person, but your time and dollars are limited? Super Sweaterman to the rescue! He's irresistibly soft: a perfect partner for TV watching or naptime. Super Sweaterman was designed with kids in mind, but he's got adult appeal too.

Materials

One pair of "toe socks" or regular knee socks: at least 15"–18" long. Find a "wild" pair, in unusual stripes, patterns, and colors.

Sweater fabric: ½ yd. Choose a soft, huggable fabric that's washable. Look in closets and drawers for recyclable old sweaters.

Polyester fiberfill: 1 lb. bag.

Lightweight nonwoven interfacing: ½ yd. for inner form casing.

Fabric scraps: For eyes, cheeks, tooth.

Yarn or embroidery floss: For hair and finishing for facial features.

Buttons: Two movable, toy eyes.

1. Cut out Sweaterman's face and hands from the sweater fabric. Add ⅝" for seams on all pattern sides. Using the circular body as a pattern, cut out the inner casing from lightweight nonwoven interfacing.

2. Cut each sock into two lengths: 10"–12" for legs; 5"–8" for arms. Vary the lengths as desired.

3. Sew the hand pieces together by hand and then join to the shorter sock (arm) lengths. Don't forget to make a right and a left thumb.

4. Stuff the arms and legs until they're filled out but still soft. Sew across the raw edges on all arm and leg pieces to hold in the stuffing.

5. Embroider Sweaterman's face: mark all facial lines with basting first. An embroidery hoop helps keep the stitches straight. Use yarn or embroidery floss for the stitching. Cross stitch the eyebrows and nose. Backstitch the smile. Blanket stitch the eyes, cheeks, and tooth.

6. Sandwich the arms and legs between the right sides of the body front and back pieces. Sew a 5/8" seam around the circular body pieces, joining the arms and legs in the seam. Leave a 3"–4" opening along one side for stuffing. Turn right sides out.

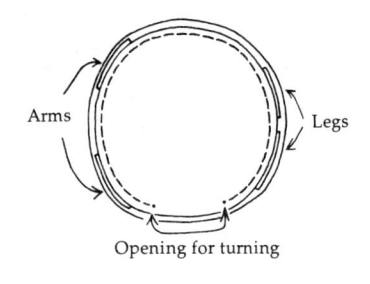

Arms   Legs

Opening for turning

7. Super Sweaterman's hair is looped fringe 2" long worked between the two arm pieces along the seam line (see page 124).

8. Sew the inner form casing, leaving a 3"–4" opening. Put the inner form casing inside Sweaterman's body. Stuff with polyester fiberfill to the "fatness" you desire.

9. Close the inner casing first and then the body opening with hand stitching.

If you make more than one Super Sweaterman (you'll be deluged with requests), you can have fun changing the facial expression, hair length, fabric texture and color—even the number of arms and legs!

Much More than Sweaters • 199

SWEATER YOUR HOME

◢. STRETCH-TO-FIT FURNITURE THROWS

There's no easier way to perk up a tired piece of furniture than to dress it up with a stretch-to-fit furniture throw. Sweater fabric by the yard eliminates the time-consuming fitting, pinning, and sewing of traditional slipcovers.

Rectangular throws stretch to fit the furniture contours. Dimensions for the two basic sizes of stretch-to-fit throws are 90" × 70" for regular chairs and loveseats, and 140" × 70" for sofas.

Materials

Sweater fabric: 2¾ yds., 62"–72" wide for chairs and loveseats. 4¼ yds., 62"–72" wide for sofas. Both throws can be made without piecing or seaming since most sweater fabrics are 62"–72" wide.

1. Cut the 70" side with the crosswise grain, the longer side with the lengthwise grain.
2. If your fabric is slightly narrower, you can trim the entire rectangle with 2"–4" fringe (see page 122).

- Try the throw on the chair or sofa before determining fringe length. Allow for hem turn-up, usually 1". Dimensions of the throw might have to be altered slightly.
- Fringing the throw is functional as well as decorative: the fringe weights the throw hem edge and prevents curling.

Tuck the throw into the furniture corners and crevices. It will soon "take on" the shape of the chair or sofa. Instant slipcovers!

◢. SWEATER BLANKETS

Because of their softness and stretchability, sweater fabrics are naturals for blankets. (See page 171 for recycled patchwork projects.) Look for sales in fabric stores and departments. Many large scale patterns and plaids that are on sale are overpowering for garments but are perfect for blankets.

There are standard blanket measurements, but you can cut them to any size. Following are the standard measurements.

STANDARD BLANKET MEASUREMENTS
(Measurements in inches)

Twin	66 × 90	
Full	80 × 90	will have to be pieced or trimmed
Queen	90 × 90	
King	108 × 90	

1. Cut out the blanket single or double layer depending upon the thickness of the fabric.

• An advantage of a double layer blanket is that any piecing seams are hidden between the layers.

2. Fringe, bind, or crochet to make decorative borders and compensate for narrow widths.

• On very loosely knitted or bulky single layer fabrics, turn up the edge ½"–1" before stitching or fringing.

You can make stadium "lap warmer" blankets too. Just cut the fabric to the length you desire. Use the fabric width as the blanket width. Finish with fringe, binding, or crochet.

SWEATER PILLOWS

Pillows add warmth, color, and comfort to any room in your house. If it seems there's never enough of them, you can have mounds of beautiful pillows—they're inexpensive when you make your own! You don't have enough furniture? Make super big pillows for floor cushions! Use sweater fabric or yarn scraps to make pillows in all shapes and sizes.

There are many commercial patterns available for pillows, but most pillows are variations on a square or a rectangle. By varying sweater fabric selections, corner treatments, and finishing touches, you can create rooms of unique pillows—all from the same basic shape.

FABRIC FOR SWEATER PILLOWS

Sources for sweater fabric are just about limitless. Just keep in mind that fabric bought or made for any home furnishing should be cleanable, durable, colorfast, snag and pill resistant. If the pillows are for a child's room, select washable yarns and fabrics.

Your scrap bins are an excellent source for suitable sweater fabric. So are recyclable old sweaters. You can create sweater fabric for pillows by crocheting or knitting to fit. Experiment with yarns, needle or hook sizes, and stitch patterns.

Create interesting textures by combining yarn with twine and jute in crochet/knit patterns. Tightly knitted or crocheted fabric can be sewn by machine into pillow shapes. More loosely knitted, lacy constructions can be sewn or crocheted together by hand.

Or you can make patchwork pillow fabric from recyclable sweaters. (See page 171 for patchwork techniques.)

Since most sweater fabric is more "open" than wovens, covered inner pillow forms are recommended. They'll even out stuffing lumpiness, prevent the escape of stuffing, and make laundering easier. Also, without the protection of the inner pillow casing, sweater fabric sticks to the pillow stuffing.

Pillow forms and casings can be made or purchased. Here are some tips on casings and fillings.

MAKE YOUR OWN PILLOW FORM CASING

You can make your own pillow form casing and then stuff it. Although most needlecraft books and magazines suggest unbleached muslin for the pillow form casing, you'll find nonwoven interfacing (not fusible!) easier to handle. It doesn't ravel and can be cut economically because there's no grain.

1. Cut the casing 1" wider and longer than the finished pillow size. Stitch a ½" seam around casing leaving an opening large enough to stuff with the filling (approximately 4"). The casing should be slightly larger than the finished pillow in order to achieve well-stuffed corners.

2. On most pillows, the nonwoven casing doesn't even have to be turned before being stuffed since the edges won't ravel and help to fill out the pillow corners. Place the casing inside the pillow cover before you stuff it. Close the opening with a blind stitch or slipstitch.

There are inexpensive stuffings or fillers available in most needlework, fabric, department, and dime stores.

PURCHASED FORMS

These forms are most commonly stuffed with foam chips or polyester fiberfill. Avoid kapok, because it mats and becomes lumpy. Down is luxuriously soft and durable, but is expensive.

FILLERS

Don't underfill the pillow; it will look cheap and limp. Yet, overstuffing results in too-hard, sandbag pillows.

The most popular and easiest to use filler/stuffing is *polyester fiberfill*. Usually sold in 1-lb. bags, it looks like surgical cotton. It won't cling, mat, fly, or lump, and is relatively inexpensive. You can stuff pillow forms before or after placing them inside the finished pillow, but you'll put less strain on the pillow zipper or opening if you stuff the form after it's inside the pillow.

Foam pillow forms are sold in many dime stores. Since the edges on these forms are uncomfortably sharp, you'll have a smoother, more comfortable pillow if you wrap the form with a layer of polyester fiberfill before covering with the casing.

Foam slabs can be cut to size with an electric knife or serrated-edge knife. Cover slabs of foam (sold in varying thicknesses and densities) with non-woven interfacing.

Polystyrene beans are used for giant "bean bag" chairs but aren't recommended for small pillows because they tend to compress and are messy to handle.

Foam chips are springy and light, but are unmanageably clingy and hard to handle.

Feathers are soft and make excellent stuffings, but they're expensive. If you use feathers, stuff the casing over a bathtub, away from any draft (feathers fly everywhere!). An old down comforter or sleeping bag can be recycled into the stuffing for several pillows.

FASTENERS IN PILLOW COVERS

Pillow covers need to be laundered occasionally, so it's a good idea to insert fasteners along one seam edge for easy removal.

Zippers are the best fasteners for sweater pillows. For some styles and sweater fabrics, an invisible zipper is more appropriate, although a regular, double-lap zipper application is usually suitable (see page 81).

For very heavy, loosely knit or crocheted sweater fabrics, a zipper can be too bulky. In that case, slipstitch the pillow opening after stuffing with the inner form. Just remember that the pillow has to be resewn after each cleaning.

Avoid self-grip fasteners for sweater pillow closures: they catch and pull sweater fabrics and tend to be bulky.

Zippers in bulky-textured pillows

To minimize bulk on the pillow edge, insert the zipper in the back pillow section instead of in an edge seam. Sew in the zipper *before* joining the front and back sections.

1. Lay out pillow back fabric double layer. Fold pillow front in half to use as the pattern for the back, but add ⅝" seam allowances along the folded edge.
2. Insert the zipper (it should be 2"–3" shorter than the seam length) in the center back seam line. Use a double-lap zipper application (see page 81) or invisible zipper.
3. Then sew around the pillow, right sides together. Turn right sides out, through the zipper opening.

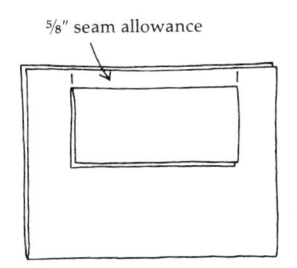

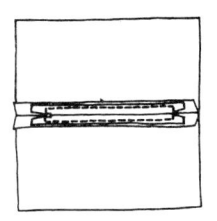

⅝" seam allowance

This back zipper method is more visible, but less bulky along the pillow edge and won't interfere with fringing or cording edge finishes.

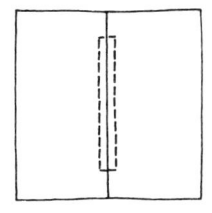

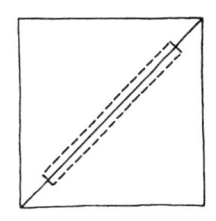

◣. SQUARE-CORNERED PILLOWS

The most common pillow corner is square and knife-edged.

1. Cut out (or crochet or knit) the pillow fabric and inner casing front and back, adding ⅝" seam allowances.

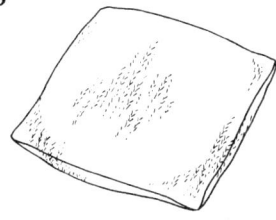

2. Sew the inner form, leaving an opening for stuffing.

3. Insert the zipper in one of the pillow seams.

4. Sew around the pillow.

• To keep the pillow corners from curling, sew the square corners at a slight curve. Take 2–3 stitches diagonally, across the corner. The corner will turn easily and lie flat.

5. Turn the pillow right side out through the zipper opening.

6. Place the inner casing inside the pillow and stuff. Sew the casing opening.

POUCHY PILLOWS

Found in many decorator showrooms, this pillow has unusual gathered corners. Pouchy pillows are an exotic change of pace from knife-edged square pillows.

Make pouchy pillows out of loosely knitted or crocheted fabric that tends to curl when sewn into regular square corners. Pouchy pillows are great as large in-place-of-furniture floor pillows.

1. Cut out (or crochet or knit) two squares or rectangles of sweater fabric and corresponding inner form casing, adding 5/8" seam allowances.

2. Sew the inner casing.

• The inner pillow form's square corners will stuff into the rounded corners of the outer pillow.

3. Insert the zipper in one of the pillow seams. The zipper should be at least 3" shorter than the pillow seam.

4. Stitch around the remaining sides of the pillow.

5. When the pillow is completely seamed and still wrong side out, tie off each corner with ordinary string 1" in from the seam pivot points.

• Avoid heavy jute or twine as it makes the corners too bulky.

Diagonally stitched corner
Trim corner after stitching

Wrong side

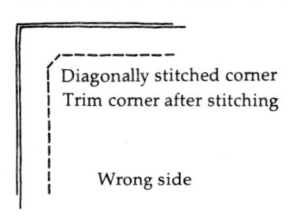

7. Zip the pillow closed and you have a square sweater pillow!

Even this most basic pillow shape can be the pattern for a houseful of cushions. Vary the fabric or edge techniques. Or add trim or embroidery.

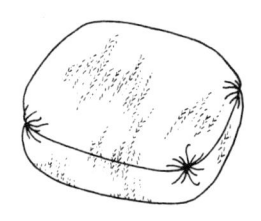

Wrong side

6. Turn the pillow right side out.

7. Place the inner pillow casing inside. Stuff and handstitch the casing opening.

◥. PERSIAN PILLOWS

Here's a corner treatment that transforms the traditional square pillow into a Persian pillow. Because of the pleated Persian corners, fabrics for these pillows should be firm, and not too bulky or lacy. Test a sample of the fabric; does it form a smooth, flat pleat?

1. Cut out (or crochet or knit) two squares or rectangles of sweater fabric the desired pillow size plus 5/8" seam allowances. Cut out two squares or rectangles of casing.

2. Sew the inner form casing with regular square corners, leaving an opening for stuffing.

3. Mark a square on the right side of each corner of the pillow fabric using the outer edges as two of the sides.

• Squares of 2 5/8" (2 high + 5/8" seam allowances) create a 4" high finished pillow.

4. Work on one corner at a time. Bring points A and C together, forming the Persian pleats on the right side of the fabric. Baste in place along the seam lines. Continue until all eight corners are pleated.

5. Insert the zipper in one pillow seam.

6. Stitch the remaining seams, right sides together, matching all pleated corners.

7. Turn the pillow to the right side through the zipper opening. Put the inner pillow form inside.

8. Stuff and close the casing opening with hand whipstitching.

The result is a posh Persian pillow!

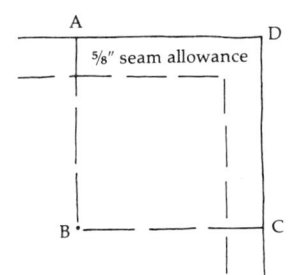

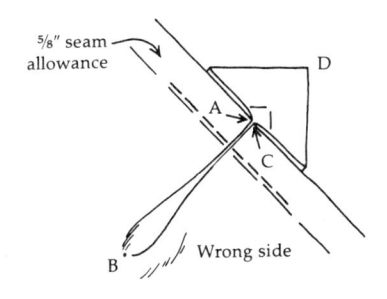

The softness of pouchy pillows makes them naturals for sweater fabric coverings—even very bulky, jacquard types.

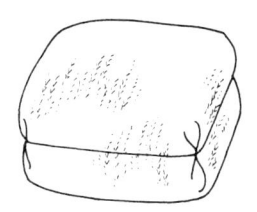

3-D PILLOWS

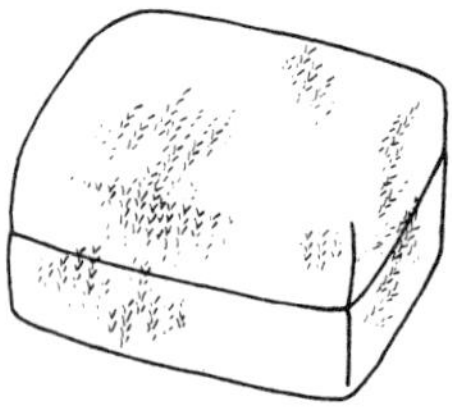

3-D corners are similar to Persian pillow corners, but the pleat is stitched in place. When you make casing covers for foam slabs, you'll find 3-D corners particularly useful.

1. Follow Steps 1, 2, 3, and 4 for the square pillow.
5. Press open the seams. Then fold the corner, aligning seam to seam.
6. Square off the first corner by stitching across the corner, perpendicular to the pillow seams. Backstitch.
   • The height of the pillow equals the length of this stitching line.
7. Trim off the corner to minimize bulk.
8. Continue to square off the other three corners. Turn.
9. Stuff with the inner form.

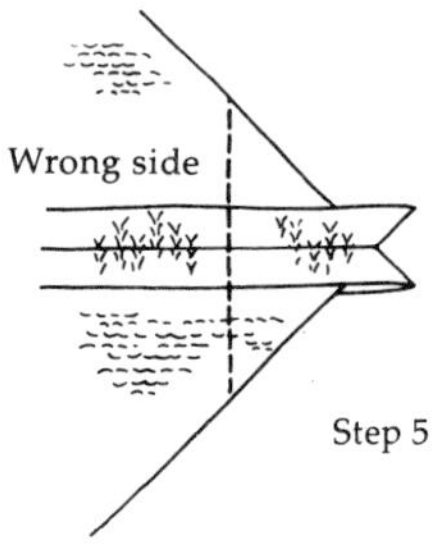

Step 5

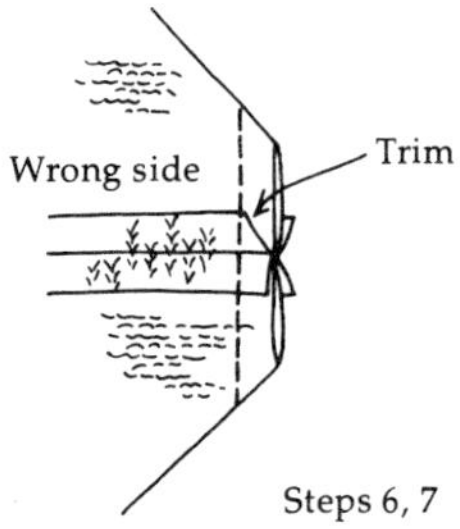

Steps 6, 7

FRINGED PILLOWS

Vary any of the basic pillow designs with fringe! None of your houseguests will ever guess they're all the same design, cleverly disguised with fringing. Don't stop there: have fun with fringe and create your own designer originals. (See page 122 for fringing instructions.)

There are so many ways to decorate with fringe. . . . Try fringing the outer edges of pillows or just one edge for an asymmetrical look. Play with checkerboard pattern fringe, or long and short fringe, or how about the rug look with row after row of fringe. See page 173 for a photo of a fringed pillow.

APPENDIX

CARE AND STORAGE OF SWEATER CRAFT GARMENTS

Sweater craft items, both ready-made and hand-crafted, should be given special care. In general, avoid storing stretchable sweater craft garments on hangers. Carefully fold sweaters after wearing. To prevent pilling and snagging, turn sweaters inside out when storing.

Inexpensive, clear plastic boxes are great for storing sweater craft items. Plastic boxes are smooth (unlike some wood drawers that can catch and snag sweaters) and are both moth and mildew proof. And it's easy to see your sweaters!

For summer storage, moth balls are recommended for wool sweaters, blankets, and afghans. Be sure to launder sweaters before storing so they will not retain odors or stains.

Do not store sweater projects or fabrics near windows because they might fade. And avoid tight plastic bags; sweaters can't breathe in them and might get permanently musty.

LAUNDERING SWEATER CRAFT GARMENTS

Whether you dry clean or wash your sweater craft garments depends primarily on the fiber content. (See the chart, Sweater Fabric Fiber Content, page 25.)

DRY CLEANING

Ask your dry cleaner to measure your sweater craft garments before cleaning and have him block them to the same shape afterwards.

WASHING

When you launder sweaters at home—especially those made of linen, cotton, wool, and rayon—it's a good idea to take a few quick measurements beforehand; that is, sleeve and bodice length, bust and hip width, cuff, and neckline. Then when you lay out the sweater to dry, shape it to those measurements.

Acrylics have excellent "shape memory" and return to their original size after being washed and tumble dried.

Turn the sweater inside out before washing to minimize abrasion and pilling. Dissolve mild detergent or soap in cold to lukewarm water before putting in the sweater. Don't use too much soap! Swish the sweater around in the suds but keep it under water. Pulling the sweater in and out of the water will stretch it. Avoid rubbing parts of the sweater together since this causes pilling. Allow the sweater to soak for only a few minutes, *not hours!* Lengthy soaking could cause colors to run.

Thorough rinsing is fundamental to thorough cleaning. Rinse at least four times in cold water. Don't hold the wet sweater up out of the water because it will sag. Twisting and wringing are taboo—squeeze the sweater gently instead. Roll the sweater up in a colorfast towel.

Some sweaters can be washed by machine. Follow manufacturer's instructions.

Dry the sweater flat on a dry towel or a flat sweater rack, away from direct sun and heat. Size it to the original measurements while it's still damp. Do not hang to dry. To speed up the drying process, change the towel two or three times and turn the sweater.

Touch-up pressing may be necessary after drying; press on the wrong side. Iron temperature should be adjusted for the fiber content. (Refer to the chart, Sweater Fabric Fiber Content, page 25.)

PILLING POINTERS

Pilling plagues sweaters of all kinds, from the most exclusive to the least expensive. Turning sweaters inside out when laundering helps to prevent pilling, but won't completely stop the little balls from forming.

If your sweater fabric is pill-prone, brush it with a hard brush *in one direction.* As a last resort, trim off the pill balls with a straight-edge razor, being careful not to cut the sweater itself.

SWEATERS: FIRST CLASS PASSENGERS

Sweaters are perfect traveling companions because they are wrinkle-resistant. To prevent creases, fold sweaters along seam lines. Place other garments between sweater folds; there'll be no need for touch-up pressing when you arrive at your destination. Fold garments for long-term storage in this same manner.

ENLARGING OR REDUCING DESIGNS

Determine how much to enlarge or reduce the design by considering the size of the completed project and the size relationship between the completed size and the design size.

Place a grid over the design. The grid should consist of carefully measured exact squares.

Prepare a grid with the same number of squares as the grid superimposed over the design. Number the squares along one side and the top of both grids for easy reference while drawing.

To enlarge design: The prepared grid should have larger squares than the original design. If the design to be enlarged is superimposed with a grid of ⅛" squares, translate it onto a grid of ¼", ½", or 1" squares.

To reduce design: The prepared grid should have smaller squares than the original design. If the design to be reduced is superimposed with a grid of 1" squares, translate it onto a grid of ½", ¼", or ⅛" squares.

Note: A short cut is to overlay the original design with graph paper or fine wire screen. The design may be drawn onto the graph paper, so that the need to painstakingly construct grids is eliminated.

Translate the original outline to the grid one square at a time.

METRIC EQUIVALENCY CHART
CONVERTING INCHES TO CENTIMETERS AND YARDS TO METERS
This chart gives the standard equivalents as approved by the Pattern Fashion Industry

mm—millimeters   cm—centimeters   m—meters

INCHES INTO MILLIMETERS AND CENTIMETERS
(SLIGHTLY ROUNDED FOR YOUR CONVENIENCE)

inches	mm		cm	inches	cm	inches	cm
⅛	3			7	18	29	73.5
¼	6			8	20.5	30	76
⅜	10	or	1	9	23	31	79
½	13	or	1.3	10	25.5	32	81.5
⅝	15	or	1.5	11	28	33	84
¾	20	or	2	12	30.5	34	86.5
⅞	22	or	2.2	13	33	35	89

METRIC EQUIVALENCY CHART

INCHES INTO MILLIMETERS AND CENTIMETERS

inches	mm		cm	inches	cm	inches	cm
1	25	or	2.5	14	35.5	36	91.5
1¼	32	or	3.2	15	38	37	94
1½	38	or	3.8	16	40.5	38	96.5
1¾	45	or	4.5	17	43	39	99
2	50	or	5	18	46	40	101.5
2½	65	or	6.5	19	48.5	41	104
3	75	or	7.5	20	51	42	106.5
3½	90	or	9	21	53.5	43	109
4	100	or	10	22	56	44	112
4½	115	or	11.5	23	58.5	45	114.5
5	125	or	12.5	24	61	46	117
5½	140	or	14	25	63.5	47	119.5
6	150	or	15	26	66	48	122
				27	68.5	49	124.5
				28	71	50	127

YARDS INTO METERS
(SLIGHTLY ROUNDED FOR YOUR CONVENIENCE)

Yards	Meters	Yards	Meters	Yards	Meters	Yards	Meters	Yards	Meters
⅛	.15	2⅛	1.95	4⅛	3.80	6⅛	5.60	8⅛	7.45
¼	.25	2¼	2.10	4¼	3.90	6¼	5.75	8¼	7.55
⅜	.35	2⅜	2.20	4⅜	4.00	6⅜	5.85	8⅜	7.70
½	.50	2½	2.30	4½	4.15	6½	5.95	8½	7.80
⅝	.60	2⅝	2.40	4⅝	4.25	6⅝	6.10	8⅝	7.90
¾	.70	2¾	2.55	4¾	4.35	6¾	6.20	8¾	8.00
⅞	.80	2⅞	2.65	4⅞	4.50	6⅞	6.30	8⅞	8.15
1	.95	3	2.75	5	4.60	7	6.40	9	8.25
1⅛	1.05	3⅛	2.90	5⅛	4.70	7⅛	6.55	9⅛	8.35
1¼	1.15	3¼	3.00	5¼	4.80	7¼	6.65	9¼	8.50
1⅜	1.30	3⅜	3.10	5⅜	4.95	7⅜	6.75	9⅜	8.60
1½	1.40	3½	3.20	5½	5.05	7½	6.90	9½	8.70
1⅝	1.50	3⅝	3.35	5⅝	5.15	7⅝	7.00	9⅝	8.80
1¾	1.60	3¾	3.45	5¾	5.30	7¾	7.10	9¾	8.95
1⅞	1.75	3⅞	3.55	5⅞	5.40	7⅞	7.20	9⅞	9.05
2	1.85	4	3.70	6	5.50	8	7.35	10	9.15

AVAILABLE FABRIC WIDTHS

25"	65cm	50"	127cm
27"	70cm	54"/56"	140cm
35"/36"	90cm	58"/60"	150cm
39"	100cm	68"/70"	175cm
44"/45"	115cm	72"	180cm
48"	122cm		

AVAILABLE ZIPPER LENGTHS

4"	10cm	10"	25cm	22"	55cm
5"	12cm	12"	30cm	24"	60cm
6"	15cm	14"	35cm	26"	65cm
7"	18cm	16"	40cm	28"	70cm
8"	20cm	18"	45cm	30"	75cm
9"	22cm	20"	50cm		

SOURCES OF INFORMATION AND SUPPLIES

SWEATER CRAFT INFORMATION

National Needlework Association
National Hand Knitting Yarn Committee
230 Fifth Avenue
New York, New York 10001
  Information regarding yarn manufacturers, brand names. Educational seminars for teachers.

Coats and Clark's Sales Corp.
72 Cummings Point Road
Stamford, Connecticut 06902
  Educational pamphlets and posters on knitting, crocheting, and sewing.

DuPont Company
Textile Fibers Product Information Dept.
Centre Road Building
Wilmington, Delaware 19898
  Educational information regarding fibers and yarn. Information supplied to teachers regarding Craft Yarn teacher program.

SWEATER PATTERNS

Butterick Fashion Marketing Co.
161 Sixth Avenue
New York, New York 10013

McCall's Pattern Co.
230 Park Avenue
New York, New York 10016

Simplicity Pattern Co., Inc.
200 Madison Avenue
New York, New York 10016

Vogue Pattern Service
161 Sixth Avenue
New York, New York 10013

Stretch & Sew, Inc.
220 South Seneca Road
Eugene, Oregon 97401

Kwik-Sew Pattern Co., Inc.
300 Sixth Avenue
North Minneapolis, Minnesota 55401

Kandel Knits
4834 North Interstate Avenue
Portland, Oregon 97217

RETAIL STORES AND MAIL ORDER

These fabric retailers carry sweater knits on a seasonal basis.

Fabric Land
855 Route 22
North Plainfield, New Jersey 07060

And Sew Forth
65 East Allendale Ave.
Saddle Brook, New Jersey 07458

Kandel Knits
4834 North Interstate Ave.
Portland, Oregon 97401

Hancock Fabrics
836 Joe Clifton Road
Paducah, Kentucky 42001

Britex
14 Geary Street
San Francisco, California 94108

Check your Yellow Pages for local listings of the following retail store chains:

Cloth World
Hancock Fabrics
Mary Lester Fabrics
Minnesota Fabrics
Northwest
Stretch & Sew

SWEATER CRAFT YARN AND THREAD SUPPLIERS

American Thread Co.
High Ridge Park
Stamford, Connecticut 06905

Berga Ullman Inc.
59 Demond Avenue
N. Adams, Massachusetts 01247

Emile Bernat & Sons Co.
Depot and Mendon Street
Uxbridge, Massachusetts 01569

Brunswick Worsted Mills Inc.
230 Fifth Avenue
New York, New York 10001

Bucilla
30-20 Thompson Avenue
Long Island City, New York 11101

Coats & Clark's Sales Corp.
72 Cummings Point Road
Stamford, Connecticut 06902

Columbia-Minerva Corp.
295 Fifth Avenue
New York, New York 10016

Craft Yarn Teacher Program
  (Teachers only)
DuPont Company
Textile Fibers Product Information
Centre Road Building
Wilmington, Delaware 19898

DuPont Company
Textile Fibers Product Information
Centre Road Builing
Wilmington, Delaware 19898

D.M.C. Corp.
107 Trumbull Street
Elizabeth, New Jersey 07206

Folklorico Yarn Co.
522 Ramona Street
Palo Alto, California 94301

Lion Brand Yarn Company
1270 Broadway
New York, New York 10001

Malina
1071 Ave. of the Americas
New York, New York 10018

Melrose Yarn Company Inc.
1305 Utica Avenue
Brooklyn, New York 11203

National Needlework Association
National Hand Knitting Yarn Committee
230 Fifth Avenue
New York, New York 10001

Needlecraft Corp. of America
3900 N. Claremont Avenue
Chicago, Illinois 60618

Plymouth Yarn Company
500 Lafayette Street
Bristol, Pennsylvania 19007

Reynolds Yarns Inc.
15 Oser Avenue
Hauppague, New York 11787

Spinnerin Yarn Co.
230 Fifth Avenue
New York, New York 10001

Stanley Berroco, Inc.
140 Mendon Street
Uxbridge, Massachusetts 01569

Tahki Imports Ltd.
62 Madison Street
Hackensack, New Jersey 07601

William Unger & Co.
230 Fifth Avenue
New York, New York 10001

SWEATER CRAFT NOTIONS

Boye Needle Co.
916 South Arcade
Freeport, Illinois 61032

C. J. Bates and Son Inc.
Route 9A
Chester, Connecticut 06412

Belding Lily Co.
P.O. Box 88
Shelby, North Carolina 28150

Dritz
Division of Scovill Mfg. Co.
Buckingham Street
Watertown, Connecticut 06795

Talon
41 East 51st Street
New York, New York 10022

SWEATER CRAFT TRIMS

William E. Wright
1 Penn Plaza
New York, New York 10001

Talon
41 East 51st Street
New York, New York 10022

Coats & Clark's Sales Corp.
72 Cummings Point Road
Stamford, Connecticut 06902

Dolphin Trimming
318 NW 23rd Street
Miami, Florida 33127

INDEX

A

Accessories, 182–190
Afghans, 138, 142
Appliqué, 88, 130, 168, 175

B

Bar tacks, 86
Bedspreads
  chevron patchwork, 138
  quilted, 132
Belt, bias tube, 171
Bias
  hand-knitting or crocheting on, 165
  sweater garments on, 136, 170
  tube belt, 171
Binding
  techniques, 56–58, 128–129
  V-necks and cardigans, 67–71
  zippers, 84
Blankets
  baby, 191
  sweater, 199–200
Blanket stitch, how to, 119–120
Blocking, 153
Boat neck, 50–51, 64–66
Body fit, 18, 38
Borders, striped, 137
Braid
  edging, 58–61
  monograms, 88
Buttonholes, 101, 119, 128
Buttons, loops for, 102

C

Cardigans
  construction, 56–57, 59, 71–73
  laying out, 42–43, 45
  T-sweater, 101
Care
  for fibers, 25–31
  sweater garments, 207–208
Casings, 62–64, 113, 200–206

Catch stitch, how to, 77
Circumference, fitting, 32, 36, 38
Closures, types, 101–103
  see also Buttonholes, Buttons, *and* Zippers
Cording, 114, 167
Cowl necklines, 95
Crewneck, 15, 50–51, 64–66
Crocheting
  basics, 154–155, 157–158
  edging and trim, 62, 120–121
  garments, 141–167
  seams, 89–90
  see also Hand-knitting and crocheting
Cuffs, 78–79
Cutting sweater fabrics, 45

D

Decorative
  closures, 102–103, 113–114
  edging, 117–127
  seams, 89–94
  zippers, 82–83
Decreasing, hand-knitting and crocheting, 158–160
Designing sweater garments, 87–140

E

Ease allowance
  design, relation to, 17–18, 38
  pattern, determining from, 37
Ease plus, technique, 52–53
Edging techniques, 117–127
Elastic, in casing, 62–64

F

Fabric components, 20
Fiber content, 14, 24–31
Fiberfill batting, 202
  see also Pillows *and* Quilting

Fitting adjustments
  for children, 39
  circumference, 38
  hand-knitted or crocheted garments, 152
  length, 32, 38–39, 43, 140
  minimizing, 14, 35
  miter, centering, 69
  pattern measurements, 37
  ribbing, 165
Flouncing, 76
Fringe, 122–127, 206
Front closure styles, 52
Full fit
  ease, guidelines, 38
  maternity tops, 140
  pattern design, 18
  sweater jacket, lined, 131
Fur, 128–130

G

Golf club mitts, 189–191
Grain
  bias, 57–58, 136
  straightening, 40–43

H

Hand-knitting
  basics, 56–57
  on bias, 165
  casings, 64
  edgings, 121–122
  ribbing, 163, 165
  yokes, circular, 97
Hand-knitting and crocheting
  assembling, 162–163
  stitch pattern, selection, 145–146
  stitch gauge, 146–147
  T-sweaters, 163–164
  tools, 142–143
Hats
  trimming, 128–129
  tube, 183–184
Headband, 186–187
Hems, 74–77
Home furnishings
  ideas and construction, 199–206

quilting, 134
from recycled fabrics, 171–174

I

Increasing
  circumference, 38
  in hand-knitting and crocheting, 158–160
  length, 39
Inserts
  on T-sweater, 100
  lace, 92–93

K

Keyhole neckline, 97
Knit stitches, 19–23

L

Lace, 92–94
Leather
  buttonhole lips, 101, 116
  closures, in and out, 114
  lacing, 114, 129
  patches, for mending, 179–180
  on pillows, 195
  on sweater garments, 128–130
  ties, braided thong, 103–104
  toggles, 102
Long John seam, 90–91

M

Machine, sewing, 46–48
Macrame, 62, 113
Marking, sweater fabrics, 45–46
Maternity tops, 140
Measurements
  bedspreads, chart, 172
  blankets, chart, 200
  body, in relation to pattern, 32–37, 150–151
  cowl collar, 95
  fringe, 123–127
  throws, furniture, 199
Mending, 18, 178–179
Metric equivalency chart, 209–210

Mitering
  centering, 69
  technique, 56–57
  in trim application, 60–62
Mittens, cut and sewn, 192–193
Monograms, 88–89, 167

N

Nap, in pattern layout, 43
Neck warmers, 185
Neckline, *see individual neckline styles*

P

Patchwork
  chevron, 134, 138–139
  leather, 130
  recycled sweater fabric, 171, 174
Pattern
  commercial sewing, 17–19, 152–153
  coordination with fabric, 13
  enlarging or reducing, 209
  European, 151
  graphing, 149–151
  for pom-poms, 125–126
  preparation, 35–40
  ready-to-wear, making from, 40
  selection, 13, 149
  size, 14, 32–34
Pattern layout
  adjustments, 38–39
  on the bias, 136
  cardigans, 42–43, 45
  chevron patchwork, 139
  extra wide double layer, 42
  hand-knitted or crocheted garments, 43–44
  in pattern making, 40
  for pile stretch knits, 22
  pullovers, 42–43
  recycled fabrics, 44
  rules for, 41–45
  stripes, matching, 133–136
  sweater bodies, 43
  sweater fabric by the yard, 43
Pilling, 144, 208
Pillows, 200–206
  for children, 194–198
Pockets, 85–86, 116, 182, 189

Pom-poms, 125–127
Purses, 188–189

Q

Quilting, 132, 173–174

R

Ribbing, as edging, 55–56
Recycled fabrics
  cutting, 43
  how to use, 168–180
  ideas for, 181–206
  pattern layout, 45
  selection and souces, 16
Restyling, 16, 168–180
Ribbon edging
  applying, 59–61
  on cardigans, 71–73

S

Seams
  decorative handcrafted, 89–90
  sweater, 53–54
Skirt, hand-knitted, 42
Sleeves
  construction shortcuts, 50–52
  pattern, making for, 40
  raglan, 98
  see also T-sweaters
Smocking, 116–117
Spool cording, 167
Square neckline, 97–98
Stitch in the ditch binding, 57–58
Stitch gauge, for hand-knitted and crocheted garments, 145–149, 151–152
"Stitch to row", 90
Stretch gauge, 17–19
Stretchability
  coordination with pattern, 13, 32
  degrees, 14
  determining, 17
  fiber content, effect of, 24
  of knit stitches, 20–23
Stripes, 133–137, 100
Style, selection, 13
Supplies, sources, 211–212

Sweater bodies, 15, 43, 63, 187–188
Sweater fabric by the yard, 14–15, 43, 63

T

T-sweaters
  cardigan, 101
  construction, 99–101, 163
  hand-knitted or crocheted, 163
  with insert, 100
  racing stripe, 100
  seamed, split front and back, 100
  "sew simple", 101
Tassels, 122–127
  "no hassle", 127
Throws, furniture, 199–200
Toggle closures, 59, 71, 102
Tools, for knitting and crocheting, 142–144, 148
Tubular articles, 142, 180
Turtleneck (and mock turtle)
  construction, 50–51
  finishes, 66
  tight, tall, 66–67
  variations, 95
Transfers, iron-on, 174–175
Trim, 58–62

U

Underbody fit
  coordination with pattern style, 13
  ease for, 38
  lace inserts in, 93

W

Waistband
  drawstring, 113
  elasticized, 62
  increasing or decreasing, 38
  measuring, 33–34
  ribbing, contour-fit, 152
Weft knit, 20
Woven fabric, combined with knits, 57, 130, 132, 166
Wrist warmers, 185–186

Y

Yarn
  monograms, 88
  selection, 118, 120, 144–145
Yoke, circular, 96–97

Z

Zippers
  in designing garments, 115
  in pillows, 174, 202–205
  selection and installation, 81–83